A Prayer Book for

REMEMBERING
THE WOMEN

A Prayer Book for
REMEMBERING
THE WOMEN

FOUR SEVEN-DAY CYCLES OF PRAYER
Anointing Women
Women Evangelists and Apostles
Holy Wisdom
The Creator and Creation

J. Frank Henderson

Hymn texts by Mary Louise Bringle

LTP

LITURGY
TRAINING
PUBLICATIONS

ACKNOWLEDGMENTS

Other Books by J. Frank Henderson Available from LTP
Remembering the Women
Liturgies of Lament
A Triduum Sourcebook (with Joan Halmo)

Canticles and readings are taken from the *New Revised Standard Version Bible,* copyright 1989, Division of Christian Education of the National Council of the Churches of Christ in the United States of America. Used by permission. All rights reserved. Psalms are taken from the revised Grail translation, copyright 1963, 1986, 1993 by Ladies of the Grail (England). Used by permission of GIA Publications, Inc., exclusive agent. All rights reserved. The English translation of the Song of Mary used here was prepared by the English Language Liturgical Consultation (ELLC) in 1988. These sources use language that is generally inclusive. In some instances biblical texts have been further emended according to the principles published in the *Lectionary for the Christian People* and more recently in *Readings for the Assembly.*

Format and text selection © 2001 J. Frank Henderson.

Hymn texts © 2001 Mary Louise Bringle.

A PRAYER BOOK FOR REMEMBERING THE WOMEN © 2001 Archdiocese of Chicago: Liturgy Training Publications, 1800 North Hermitage Avenue, Chicago IL 60622-1101; 1-800-933-1800; fax 1-800-933-7094; orders@ltp.org; www.ltp.org. All rights reserved.

This book was edited by Gabe Huck with assistance from Lorie Simmons. Bryan Cones was the production editor. The cover was designed by Lucy Smith. The interior design is by Larry Cope and is based on an original design by Lisa Buckley. The typesetting was done by Karen Mitchell in Trajan and Stempel Garamond. The cover and interior art is by Luba Lukova. The book was printed by Von Hoffmann Graphics, Inc., of Eldridge, Iowa.

Library of Congress Cataloging-in-Publication Data

Henderson, J. Frank (Joseph Frank), 1933–
    A prayer book for remembering the women : four seven-day cycles of prayer / J. Frank Henderson; hymn texts by Mary Louise Bringle.
      p. cm.
    ISBN 1-56854-314-X
    1. Bible—Prayers. 2. Women—Prayer-books and devotions—English. 3. Women in the Bible. 4. Bible and feminism. I. Bringle, Mary Louise. II. Title.

BV228 .H45 2001
242'.8—dc21

2001038730

CONTENTS

2   *Introduction*

13   *Preparation Rites*

ANOINTING WOMEN   17

18   *Morning Prayer*

38   *Evening Prayer*

WOMEN EVANGELISTS AND APOSTLES   59

60   *Morning Prayer*

77   *Evening Prayer*

HOLY WISDOM   99

100   *Morning Prayer*

120   *Evening Prayer*

THE CREATOR AND CREATION   141

142   *Morning Prayer*

162   *Evening Prayer*

INTRODUCTION

THE PASCHAL MYSTERY

In Christian liturgical tradition, Morning Prayer and Evening Prayer celebrate the paschal mystery of Jesus Christ—incarnation, death, resurrection and sending of the Spirit. Christ's paschal mystery infuses the life of the church in every place, every age, every moment. But we know these deeds in the context of the stories told by the scriptures. That context does not limit the meaning and significance of the paschal mystery to a particular time and place; entering into these stories ourselves can help us understand and appreciate the paschal mystery in our lives today. These celebrations of Morning Prayer and Evening Prayer allow us to savor the scriptural context of the paschal mystery.

ANOINTING WOMEN

All four evangelists tell stories of Jesus sharing a meal at someone's home when a loving and courageous woman anointed him with precious ointment. In Matthew, Mark and John, this anointing anticipates Jesus' death and burial. Because this anointing took place at the dinner table, it must have been late afternoon or evening.

Luke's gospel recounts how some women prepared spices and ointments after the crucifixion. They rested on the Sabbath day. On the morning of the first day of the week they approached the tomb, carrying these spices and ointments, so that they might properly bury Jesus' body. This was an act of love, fidelity and courage. In different biblical accounts, the women are told that Jesus has risen, or they experience the risen Christ themselves. They are then commissioned to carry this good news to the other disciples.

These women were not alone in their fidelity. Mary the mother of Jesus and other women also stood near the cross and then the tomb; they kept vigil. At Pentecost, these women disciples were among those filled with the Holy Spirit.

All of these stories are pondered and celebrated here in the order of prayer titled "Anointing Women."

WOMEN EVANGELISTS AND APOSTLES

The close relationship between Jesus and women demonstrated in the stories of his death and resurrection reminds us of Jesus' relationships with women throughout the gospel stories. In his ministry to them, women were raised up, affirmed and empowered. Here, some of these women are considered to be "evangelists" (tellers of good news) inasmuch as they communicated the good news of Jesus' ministry.

In the early decades of the church, women heard and responded to the preaching of the good news and received the new life of Christ and the Holy Spirit through baptism. They cared for the ecclesial body of Christ in many ways, including serving as community leaders. Here, some of these women are considered to be "apostles" because they spread the good news and provided leadership in the early church.

We also remember women of the Hebrew scriptures, who were the foremothers of Jesus and the early church.

Jesus' relationships with women affirm that both women and men are made in the image and likeness of God. We also see the feminine face of God already expressed in the Hebrew scriptures. These scriptures and the full range of images of God contained in them were Jesus' inheritance; he declared that not one jot or tittle of them should be changed.

These stories and images are pondered and celebrated here in the order of prayer titled "Women Evangelists and Apostles."

HOLY WISDOM

The figure of Holy Wisdom persists through the centuries, before Jesus and after. She is a feminine image of God or of God's companion, and of God's presence to humankind. The image of Holy Wisdom is rich and multifaceted, far beyond the scope of our English word "wisdom." Today we are beginning to appreciate Wisdom's significance. In the Christian scriptures, Jesus assumes much of the persona and ministry of Holy Wisdom, though in this process wisdom's feminine dimension has often been diminished or lost.

The biblical canticles that celebrate Holy Wisdom are not prominent in the traditional Christian liturgy. Here, these canticles and related scripture texts have been used in an order of prayer titled "Holy Wisdom."

THE CREATOR AND CREATION

Morning and evening are times when we are particularly conscious of creation, and it is natural for the church to praise the Creator at the beginning and end of each day. In an earlier time, the hymns of Evening Prayer every day recounted the Genesis story of that day's creation. In Christian tradition, Easter is the first day of a new creation, and that awareness permeates both Morning Prayer and Evening Prayer.

Psalms and other scripture texts that proclaim the Creator and give thanks for creation have been used in an order of prayer titled "The Creator and Creation."

USERS AND USES

These four orders of Morning Prayer and Evening Prayer are offered here for the use of the church in the new millennium. They are simple, relatively brief and readily adaptable.

These rites are intended for use by the entire church—an inclusive church. Though the texts refer frequently to biblical women and feminine images of

God from the Bible, they are for both women and men. Biblical women are examples for men as well as women, and for their own spiritual benefit men need to hear and respond to the biblical stories of women that have been neglected by the church for so long. Obviously, biblical women and their stories are highly significant today for women in the church.

The orders of prayer offered here can be used by communities or by individuals. Any one of them can be used for a one-time occasion or several can be used for a series of gatherings. They can also be used as presented here, each of the four themes making a single week of prayers for morning and evening.

The rites included here may be used as they are, but their individual elements may also be approached as resources, models, suggestions and options. Sometimes material given here for a morning will be useful for evening prayer. Sometimes a text assigned here for Monday will be the right text for a gathering on a Friday. Those praying regularly at morning and evening will want to find a steady pattern and stick with it, however, so as to be free to enter the prayer.

Morning and Evening Prayer, like all liturgy, is inherently musical, and song texts have been provided at the beginning of each order of prayer. All are written so that they may be sung to well-known tunes. In some circumstances they may simply be recited or omitted. Psalms, canticles and the Lord's Prayer may also be chanted instead of spoken.

The orders of prayer presented here are deliberate in their trinitarian orientation. In particular, the Holy Spirit plays an important role in the thanksgiving texts. A wide range of names, titles, images and attributes of God, for all three persons of the Trinity, are included in the prayers.

Note that each of the four sections begins with an overview of the composition and content of the psalms, canticles and other scriptures used in Morning and Evening Prayer.

STRUCTURE

A simple pattern has been used for these liturgies of Morning Prayer and Evening Prayer:

Opening Rites
    Preparation Rite (optional)
    Opening Verse
    Song
    Thanksgiving

Psalms and Scripture
    First Psalm/Canticle (optional)
    Silence
    Second Psalm/Canticle
    Silence
    Scripture Reading
    Silence
    Song of Hannah (morning) or Song of Mary
        (evening) with daily antiphon

Concluding Rites
    Litany of Praise (morning) or
      Intercessions (evening)
    Lord's Prayer
    Closing Prayer
    Blessing
    Sign of Peace

With each of the four cycles, the song, opening verse, first psalm/canticle, Song of Hannah or of Mary, and the concluding rites are the same for each morning or evening in a given week. The second psalm/canticle, scripture reading and antiphon for the Song of Hannah or of Mary are different for each day of that week.

OPENING RITES

These actions, verses, songs and prayers gather us—as individuals and as a community—for prayer. They should be arranged—chosen, lengthened, shortened—so that they do this. They are a transition from other daily activities to the time of prayer.

In community prayer, the preparation rite (see page 14) may be necessary simply because more time and ritual is generally required to gather a larger number of people to pray as a community in Christ. Note that these rites call on us to pray with the whole person, using the senses of sight, smell and touch, as well as speech and hearing.

The sign of the cross is always made at the beginning of prayer. Usually this gesture follows some moments of silence. Sometimes prayer begins with the kissing of an icon or other image.

The hymn may be sung even if one person is praying alone. In some traditions the hymns of Morning and Evening Prayer always conclude with a doxology. Here are two doxologies, the first in Long Meter (LM) and the second in Common Meter (CM), to use with any hymn in these orders of prayer.

> Praise God, who gives us life and breath,
> whose soaring Spirit sets us free!
> Praise Christ, who triumphs over death!
> Praise mystic, dancing harmony!
>
> LM (88.88)

> Praise God, who over darkness stirred
> with birthing, brooding grace!
> Praise living Breath and saving Word!
> We give you thanks and praise!
>
> CM (86.86)

Morning Prayer includes a prayer of thanksgiving. Its three verses begin:

> "We give you [God] thanks for . . ."
> "We give thanks for Jesus . . ."
> "We give thanks for the Holy Spirit . . ."

Evening prayer also includes a prayer of thanksgiving, inspired by the ancient Jewish form of prayer called *berakah* or "blessing." It begins and concludes with "Blessed are you, O God." Its three sections begin:

"From the beginning you [God] have . . ."
"In the course of time you gave us Jesus . . ."
"Today we are called [or another verb] by the Spirit . . ."

These prayers of thanksgiving remember appropriate stories from the Hebrew and Christian scriptures, then look to the present and the future.

When there is a group praying together, one person proclaims the three thanksgiving or blessing statements, and all the others say a refrain.

PSALMS AND SCRIPTURE

Psalms or canticles constitute the central element of Morning and Evening Prayer. The order of prayer here suggests that one psalm or canticle remain the same each day, and one psalm or canticle change from day to day. The first of these is optional in the sense that if only one psalm or canticle is recited, it is omitted.

Canticles are poetic biblical texts found outside the book of psalms. In this book, these are used to a greater extent than is now usual in the church's Liturgy of the Hours. In "Anointing Women" canticles are used in place of psalms at Evening Prayer. In "Women Evangelists and Apostles" canticles are used in place of psalms at Morning Prayer. In "Holy Wisdom" canticles are used in place of psalms at both Morning Prayer and Evening Prayer

Following ancient tradition, the Song (or Canticle) of Mary is part of the liturgy of Evening Prayer. At Morning Prayer, however, the Song of Hannah replaces the traditional Song of Zechariah. A woman's voice is therefore heard at both hours.

Psalms and canticles are divided into stanzas. When two or more pray together, it is often good to alternate stanzas with one or more voices on each of two sides. Other arrangements may be chosen.

Following Roman liturgical tradition, the scripture readings are brief, usually only a few verses, more allusions than full readings. They lay out the central features of important biblical stories without many details or expansions. As noted in the scripture citations, these brief readings often skip over verses in the full text. When several pray together, the reader may announce the reading in the usual way ("A reading from the book of Sirach") and conclude the reading by saying, "The word of the Lord." All then respond, "Thanks be to God."

Following the reading and before the Song of Hannah or of Mary, there is an antiphon that changes each day. This verse often provides its own perspective from which to pray the whole canticle and is said or sung both before and after the canticle.

All the orders of prayer note that some silence is helpful after each of the psalms and after the scripture reading. This is true even when one is praying alone.

This silence not only allows the images of psalm or scripture to take root in the one praying; it also keeps the whole prayer from being rushed.

During the season of Lent the church abstains from the joyful word "alleluia." When using these prayers during Lent, then, simply omit "alleluia" whenever it occurs.

Concluding Rites

In the morning the concluding rite begins with multiple invocations of Christ, a litany with a constant response. The prayer for evening includes the intercessory prayers with which the church always concludes the day. In both cases, those praying may choose among the possibilities given and should certainly add other invocations and intercessions.

All of these prayers are then gathered up in the Lord's Prayer. Normally this saying or chanting of the Lord's Prayer ends with "For the kingdom, the power and the glory are yours, now and forever."

When more than one person is praying, the leader may then recite the closing prayer before all join in the blessing (with the sign of the cross) and the concluding peace greeting.

Preparation Rites

Especially when several people celebrate these orders of prayer together, a brief preparation rite will often help those praying make the transition into the time of prayer. Suggestions are given here for such rites. Even when there are only a few people praying together, or even when one prays alone, some ritual of entrance into the prayer may be helpful (beyond the sign of the cross and the opening verse given in each of the orders of prayer). Such rites need not have many words. Instead, they consist of the time given to gathering, to silence, to specific deeds such as signing with water or lighting a candle. The senses of sight and smell and touch bring the whole person and whole community into the prayer.

Such preparation rites make clear that the place for prayer is important. In many cases these orders of prayer will be used in the home rather than in the church or other public place. In every case the prayer will be enhanced if the space for prayer is given some attention. This can be very simple: an appropriate image in a central place, or a candle or other object to be used in the preparation rites themselves. Often, a home, classroom, meeting room or other place has a space already set aside for prayer with images, the Bible and candles.

MORNING PRAYER

For Morning Prayer, blessed water could be present so that the preparation rite is simply the taking of water and making the sign of the cross. This can be done by all, one at a time, after those gathered recite or chant the opening verse. The water should be held in a simple and beautiful vessel, and could remain in a central place or, if this is not awkward, passed from person to person. Sometimes it can be effective to take enough water on one's hand to moisten the face, then to make the sign of the cross.

Alternatives to this water rite may suggest themselves for the particular images that guide some of the prayers in this book. For example, for the Morning Prayer of the "Anointing Women" cycle, a vessel of perfumed oil could be passed slowly from one person to another for each to smell or to rub a tiny bit of the oil into the hands or the face. Participants could anoint one another with this perfumed oil. For Morning Prayer of the "Holy Wisdom" cycle, placing a few grains of incense on burning coals may be appropriate, allowing the smoke to be seen and its scent enjoyed in silence. For Morning Prayer of "The Creator and Creation" cycle, an object symbolizing the goodness and beauty of creation might be placed in the midst of the group. If appropriate, this could be passed from person to person in silence.

EVENING PRAYER

By ancient tradition, Evening Prayer begins, as one might expect, with the lighting of candles. This is the basic suggestion for a preparation rite at Evening Prayer: kindling of light (a single beautiful candle or many candles, oil lamps, or even a fire outdoors or a fireplace inside), with some quiet surrounding the gesture and the simple, traditional verse given:

> Jesus Christ is the light of the world:
> A light no darkness can extinguish.

Sometimes individual candles are held, but this may make it difficult to hold the book of prayers.

Some of the suggestions for preparation rites at Morning Prayer given above for the individual orders of prayer may also be appropriate at Evening Prayer.

ANOINTING WOMEN

At Morning Prayer, the psalms all speak of oil, anointing or the Anointed One. The readings tell of the women who went to the tomb. Jesus is seen as the Anointed One—the Christ. The antiphons for the Song of Hannah relate to the myrrh-bearing women who are celebrated in the Orthodox liturgy.

At Evening Prayer there is a dual focus: feminine images of God in the Hebrew scriptures and the women who anointed Jesus before his death or who were present at his crucifixion. The antiphons for the Song of Mary are texts meant to be the speech or thoughts of the women who anointed Jesus. Phrases from the psalms having to do with anointing are added.

MORNING PRAYER

If a preparation rite is used, this verse is spoken or chanted:
Give thanks!
On the first day of the week, at early dawn,
the women came to the tomb,
taking the spices they had prepared.

OPENING VERSE

Do not be afraid;
I know that you are looking for Jesus,
who was crucified.
Go quickly and tell his disciples:
He has been raised from the dead.

SONG

At dawn the women made their way
with spice and sweet perfume
to where their Lord and Savior lay
enshrouded in the tomb.

Yet, myst'ry of amazing grace
to those whose hearts were grieved:
They saw their Savior face to face
and lovingly believed.

The wonder of this risen Lord
a day of joy bestows:
a table set, a cup outpoured,
whose goodness overflows.

Our ointments now to Christ we bring,
as each new dawn arrives:
The sweetness of the psalm we sing,
the spice of faithful lives.

CM (86.86)

MORNING THANKSGIVING

O God, you are the source of love.
~*Accept our morning thanks and praise.*

We give you thanks for those who are anointed
with the oil of plants and fragrances of trees
    and flowers:
for Ruth and David, for Judith and Esther,
saviors and champions of Israel.
~*Accept our morning thanks and praise.*

We give you thanks for Jesus, who is the Christ,
    the Anointed One,
whose bold women friends came with myrrh
    and ointment
and were sent forth with the gospel:
    Christ is risen!
~*Accept our morning thanks and praise.*

We give you thanks for the Holy Spirit,
sweet anointing that gives us courage.
~Accept our morning thanks and praise.

FIRST PSALM/CANTICLE

Psalm 28

Your anointed finds refuge.

To you, O LORD, I call,
my rock, hear me.
If you do not heed I shall become
like those in the grave.

Hear the voice of my pleading
as I call for help,
as I lift up my hands in prayer
to your holy place.

Do not drag me away with the wicked,
with the evildoers
who speak words of peace to their neighbors
but with evil in their hearts.

Repay them as their actions deserve
and the malice of their deeds.
Repay them for the work of their hands;
give them their deserts.
For they ignore your deeds, O LORD,
and the work of your hands.
May you ruin them and never rebuild them.

Praise to you, LORD, you have heard
my cry, my appeal.
You, LORD, are my strength and my shield;
in you my heart trusts.
I was helped, my heart rejoices
and I praise you with my song.

LORD, you are the strength of your people,
a fortress where your anointed finds refuge.
Save your people; bless Israel your heritage.
Be their shepherd and carry them for ever.

A time of silence may be observed.

SECOND PSALM/CANTICLE, READING AND ANTIPHON

The second psalm/canticle, the reading and the antiphon for the Song of Hannah are arranged according to the days of the week.

SUNDAY

Psalm 20

I know God will help the anointed.

May the LORD answer in time of trial;
may the name of Jacob's God protect you.

May God send you help from the shrine
and give you support from Zion,
remember all your offerings
and receive your sacrifice with favor.

May God give you your heart's desire
and fulfill every one of your plans.
May we ring out our joy at your victory
and rejoice in the name of our God.
May the LORD grant all your prayers.

I am sure now that the LORD
will give victory to the anointed one,
will reply from holy heaven
with a mighty, victorious hand.

Some trust in chariots or horses,
but we in the name of the LORD.
They will collapse and fall,
but we shall hold and stand firm.

Give victory to the king, O LORD,
give answer on the day we call.

A time of silence may be observed.

Matthew 28:1, 9–10

After the sabbath, as the first day of the week
was dawning, Mary Magdalene and the other
Mary went to see the tomb. Suddenly Jesus met

them and said, "Greetings!" And they came to him, took hold of his feet, and worshiped him. Then Jesus said to them, "Do not be afraid; go and tell my brothers to go to Galilee; there they will see me."

A time of silence may be observed.

Antiphon for the Song of Hannah

Go quickly and tell the others:
Christ is risen, alleluia.
They too will see him.

Continue with the Song of Hannah, page 35.

Monday

Psalm 23

God anoints my head with oil.

LORD, you are my shepherd;
there is nothing I shall want.
Fresh and green are the pastures
where you give me repose.
Near restful waters you lead me,
to revive my drooping spirit.

You guide me along the right path;
you are true to your name.
If I should walk in the valley of darkness
no evil would I fear.
You are there with your crook and your staff;
with these you give me comfort.

You have prepared a banquet for me
in the sight of my foes.
My head you have anointed with oil;
my cup is overflowing.

Surely goodness and kindness shall follow me
all the days of my life.
In the LORD'S own house shall I dwell
for ever and ever.

A time of silence may be observed.

Mark 16:1–2, 5a, 6

When the sabbath was over, Mary Magdalene,
and Mary the mother of James, and Salome
bought spices, so that they might go and anoint
him. And very early on the first day of the
week, when the sun had risen, they went to the
tomb. As they entered the tomb, they saw a
young man, dressed in a white robe. He said to
them, "Do not be alarmed; you are looking for
Jesus of Nazareth, who was crucified. He has

been raised; he is not here. Look, there is the
place they laid him."

A time of silence may be observed.

Antiphon for the Song of Hannah

Let us go, like the magi,
and bring to him an offering of myrrh,
not to him in swaddling clothes
but in his winding-sheet.

Continue with the Song of Hannah, page 35.

TUESDAY

Psalm 45:3–9a

God has anointed you with the oil of gladness.

You are the fairest of the men on earth
and graciousness is poured upon your lips,
because God has blessed you for evermore.

O mighty one, gird your sword upon your thigh;
in splendor and state, ride on in triumph
for the cause of truth and goodness and right.

Take aim with your bow in your dread
    right hand.
Your arrows are sharp, peoples fall beneath you.
The foes of the king fall down and lose heart.

Your throne, O God, shall endure for ever.
A scepter of justice is the scepter
   of your kingdom.
Your love is for justice, your hatred for evil.

Therefore God, your God, has anointed you
with the oil of gladness above other kings;
your robes are fragrant with aloes and myrrh.

A time of silence may be observed.

Mark 16:9–11

Now after Jesus rose early on the first day of
the week, he appeared first to Mary Magdalene,
from whom he had cast out seven demons. She
went out and told those who had been with him,
while they were mourning and weeping. But
when they heard that he was alive and had been
seen by her, they would not believe it.

A time of silence may be observed.

Antiphon for the Song of Hannah

The wise women followed after you in haste
   with sweet-smelling spices
and announced to your disciples, O Christ,
the glad tidings of your resurrection.

Continue with the Song of Hannah, page 35.

WEDNESDAY

Psalm 84

Look on the face of God's anointed.

How lovely is your dwelling place,
LORD, God of hosts.

My soul is longing and yearning,
is yearning for the courts of the LORD.
My heart and my soul ring out their joy
to God, the living God.

The sparrow herself finds a home
and the swallow a nest for her brood;
she lays her young by your altars,
LORD of hosts, my king and my God.

They are happy, who dwell in your house,
for ever singing your praise.
They are happy, whose strength is in you,
in whose hearts are the roads to Zion.

As they go through the Bitter Valley
they make it a place of springs,
the autumn rain covers it with blessings.
They walk with ever growing strength,
they will see the God of gods in Zion.

O LORD God of hosts, hear my prayer,
give ear, O God of Jacob.
Turn your eyes, O God, our shield,
look on the face of your anointed.

One day within your courts
is better than a thousand elsewhere.
The threshold of the house of God
I prefer to the dwellings of the wicked.

For the LORD God is a rampart, a shield.
The LORD will give us favor and glory.
The LORD will not refuse any good
to those who walk without blame.

LORD, God of hosts,
happy are those who trust in you!

A time of silence may be observed.

Luke 24:2–3, 5bc, 9

The women found the stone rolled away from
the tomb, but when they went in, they did not
find the body. "Why do you look for the living
among the dead? He is not here, but has risen."
And returning from the tomb, they told all this
to the eleven and to all the rest.

A time of silence may be observed.

Antiphon for the Song of Hannah

The angel cried out to the woman full of grace:
Rejoice, O blessed one!
For on the third day your child is risen
   from the dead.

Continue with the Song of Hannah, page 35.

THURSDAY

Psalm 92

God has poured over me fresh oil.

It is good to give thanks to the LORD,
to make music to your name, O Most High,
to proclaim your love in the morning
and your truth in the watches of the night,
on the ten-stringed lyre and the lute,
with the murmuring sound of the harp.

Your deeds, O LORD, have made me glad;
for the work of your hands I shout with joy.
O LORD, how great are your works!
How deep are your designs!
The stupid cannot know this
and the foolish cannot understand.

Though the wicked spring up like grass
and all who do evil thrive,
they are doomed to be eternally destroyed.
But you, LORD, are eternally on high.
See how your enemies perish;
all doers of evil are scattered.

To me you give the wild ox's strength;
you anoint me with the purest oil.
My eyes looked in triumph on my foes;
my ears heard gladly of their fall.
The just will flourish like the palm tree
and grow like a Lebanon cedar.

Planted in the house of the LORD
they will flourish in the courts of our God,
still bearing fruit when they are old,
still full of sap, still green,
to proclaim that the LORD is just,
my rock, in whom there is no wrong.

A time of silence may be observed.

Acts of the Apostles 1:12, 14; 2:4

Then they returned to Jerusalem from the mount
called Olivet, which is near Jerusalem, a sabbath
day's journey away. All were constantly devot-
ing themselves to prayer, together with certain
women, including Mary the mother of Jesus, as
well as his brothers. All of them were filled with

the Holy Spirit and began to speak in other languages, as the Spirit gave them ability.

A time of silence may be observed.

Antiphon for the Song of Hannah

You announced to the myrrh-bearing women:
    Rejoice!
You gave peace to your friends,
and bestowed life.

Continue with the Song of Hannah, page 35.

FRIDAY

Psalm 104:10–18

God brings fresh oil to make the face shine.

You make springs gush forth in the valleys;
they flow in between the hills.
They give drink to all the beasts of the field;
the wild asses quench their thirst.
On their banks dwell the birds of heaven;
from the branches they sing their song.

From your dwelling you water the hills;
earth drinks its fill of your gift.
You make the grass grow for the cattle
and the plants to serve our needs,

that we may bring forth bread from the earth
and wine to cheer our hearts,
oil, to make our faces shine,
and bread to strengthen our hearts.

The trees of the LORD drink their fill,
the cedars God planted on Lebanon;
there the birds build their nests;
on the treetop the stork has her home.
The goats find a home on the mountains
and rabbits hide in the rocks.

A time of silence may be observed.

John 20:1–2

Early on the first day of the week, while it was
still dark, Mary Magdalene came to the tomb
and saw that the stone had been removed from
the tomb. So she ran and went to Simon Peter
and the other disciple, the one whom Jesus
loved, and said to them, "They have taken the
Lord out of the tomb, and we do not know
where they have laid him."

A time of silence may be observed.

Antiphon for the Song of Hannah

While I was weeping at the tomb,
I saw the Anointed One, alleluia,
and he called me by name.

Continue with the Song of Hannah, page 35.

SATURDAY

Psalm 105:1–15

Do not touch my anointed one.

Alleluia!

Give thanks, and acclaim God's name,
make known God's deeds among the peoples.

O sing to the Lord, sing praise;
tell all God's wonderful works!
Be proud of God's holy name,
let the hearts that seek the LORD rejoice.

Consider the LORD, who is strong;
constantly seek God's face.
Remember the wonders of the Lord,
the miracles and judgments pronounced.

O children of Abraham, God's servant,
O children of Jacob the chosen,
this is the LORD, our God;
whose judgements prevail in all the earth.

God remembers the covenant for ever,
the promise for a thousand generations,
the covenant made with Abraham,
the oath that was sworn to Isaac.

God confirmed it for Jacob as a law,
for Israel as a covenant for ever,
and said, "I am giving you a land,
Canaan, your appointed heritage."

When they were few in number,
a handful of strangers in the land,
when they wandered from country to country,
from one kingdom and nation to another,

God allowed no one to oppress them
and admonished kings on their account.
"Do not touch those I have anointed;
do no harm to any of my prophets."

A time of silence may be observed.

John 20:11a, 16, 18

But Mary stood weeping outside the tomb. Jesus
said to her, "Mary!" She turned and said to him
in Hebrew, "Rabbouni!" (which means Teacher).
Mary Magdalene went and announced to the
disciples, "I have seen the Lord"; and she told
them that he had said these things to her.

A time of silence may be observed.

Antiphon for the Song of Hannah

Go quickly and tell the others:
Christ is risen, alleluia.
They too will see him.

Continue with the Song of Hannah.

SONG OF HANNAH   *1 Samuel 2:1b–2, 5, 7–9*

My heart exults in the LORD,
my strength is exalted in my God.
My mouth derides my enemies,
because I rejoice in my victory.

There is no Holy One like the LORD,
no one besides you;
there is no Rock like our God.

Those who were full have hired themselves out
    for bread,
but those who were hungry are fat with spoil.
The barren has borne seven,
but she who has many children is forlorn.

The LORD makes poor and makes rich;
God brings low but also exalts.
The Most High raises up the poor from the dust,
lifts the needy from the ash heap,
to make them sit with princes
and inherit a seat of honor.

For the pillars of the earth are the LORD's,
and on them God has set the world.
The Most High will guard the feet
  of the faithful ones,
but the wicked shall be cut off in darkness;
for not by might does one prevail.

The antiphon is repeated.

LITANY OF PRAISE

Response to each invocation:
  Give your church new life.

Christ, source of light:
Christ, source of life:
Christ, source of our laughter:
Christ, Spirit-filled presence among us:
Christ, strength of a new day:
Christ, joy of all who trust in you:
Christ, child of Mary:
Christ, nephew of Elizabeth:
Christ, infant joy of Anna:
Christ, waker of the dawn:
Christ, presence of glory:
Christ, light of the world:
Christ, splendid radiance of our God:
Christ, strength of your people:

LORD'S PRAYER

CLOSING PRAYER

In praise and in pleading
we lift our voices, lift our hearts to you, God.
Make strong this day those most in need
   of comfort
with some touch, some anointing,
so that every hope may be in you,
the lover of humankind.
We pray in Jesus' name,
who is Lord for ever and ever.
~Amen.

BLESSING

Let us bless the Lord.
~Thanks be to God.

SIGN OF PEACE

If a preparation rite is used, this verse is spoken or chanted:
Rejoice!
Jesus Christ is the light of the world:
A light no darkness can extinguish.

OPENING VERSE

Alleluia!
Wherever the good news is proclaimed
in the whole world,
what she has done will be told
in remembrance of her.

SONG

As ev'ning fragrance fills the air,
and twilight stars begin to glow,
our hearts recall the perfumed care
of loving women long ago.

Despite a judging world's recoil,
they felt no shame at tears they shed.
With alabaster flasks of oil
they knelt to bless Christ's feet and head.

At Calv'ry's hill, they grieved their loss
as daylight's brightness dimmed to gloom.
They kept their vigil by the cross
and carried spices to the tomb.

So God keeps vigil, hears our cries,
and comforts at a mother's breast.
God wipes all tears from crying eyes,
anointing hearts to peace and rest.

LM (88.88)

EVENING THANKSGIVING

Blessed are you, O God, who wipe away
    our tears.
~*Blessed are you, O God.*

From the beginning you have comforted us,
    O God,
like a mother hen giving refuge in the shadow
    of your wings,
and calling us to sing your praise
    among the nations.
~*Blessed are you, O God.*

In the course of time you gave us Jesus,
whose feet were bathed by a woman's tears
and whose head was anointed for his passover
with a woman's perfumed oil.
~*Blessed are you, O God.*

Today we are anointed by your Spirit
    of great abundance
to stand with all who challenge lies and work
    for justice.
~*Blessed are you, O God.*

FIRST PSALM/CANTICLE

Isaiah 49:13–18

God will remember like a mother.

Sing for joy, O heavens, and exult, O earth;
break forth, O mountains, into singing!
For the LORD has comforted the people,
and will have compassion on God's
    suffering ones.

But Zion said, "The LORD has forsaken me,
my Lord has forgotten me."
Can a woman forget her nursing child,
or show no compassion for the child
    of her womb?
Even these may forget,
yet I will not forget you.

See, I have inscribed you on the palms
    of my hands;
your walls are continually before me.
Your builders outdo your destroyers,
and those who laid you waste go away from you.

Lift up your eyes all around and see;
they all gather, they come to you.
As I live, says the LORD,
you shall put all of them on like an ornament,
and like a bride you shall bind them on.

A time of silence may be observed.

SECOND PSALM/CANTICLE, READING AND ANTIPHON

The second psalm/canticle, the reading and the antiphon for the Song of Mary are arranged according to the days of the week.

SUNDAY

Isaiah 25:6–10a

God wipes away tears.

On this mountain the LORD of hosts will make
    for all peoples
a feast of rich food, a feast of well-aged wines,
of rich food filled with marrow,
of well-aged wines strained clear.

And God will destroy on this mountain
the shroud that is cast over all peoples,
the sheet that is spread over all nations;
God will swallow up death forever.

Then the LORD God will wipe away the tears
    from all faces,
and the disgrace of the people will be taken
    away from all the earth,
for the LORD has spoken.

It will be said on that day,
Lo, this is our God, we have waited for God so
    that we might be saved.
This is the LORD for whom we have waited;
let us be glad and rejoice in the salvation
    of the LORD.
For the hand of the LORD will rest
    on this mountain.

A time of silence may be observed.

Matthew 26:7, 12–13

A woman came to Jesus with an alabaster jar of
very costly ointment, and she poured it on his
head as he sat at the table. Jesus said, "By pouring this ointment on my body she has prepared
me for burial. Truly I tell you, wherever this
good news is proclaimed in the whole world,
what she has done will be told in remembrance
of her."

A time of silence may be observed.

Antiphon for the Song of Mary

I am anointing Jesus' head with costly nard,
for he is nearing a tragic and violent death.
I am certain, however, that God will give
    victory to the Anointed One.

Continue with the Song of Mary, page 54.

MONDAY

Isaiah 42:10–12, 14–16

God cried out like a woman in labor.

Sing to the LORD a new song,
God's praise from the end of the earth!
Let the sea roar and all that fills it,
the coastlands and their inhabitants.

Let the desert and its towns lift up their voice,
the villages that Kedar inhabits;
let the inhabitants of Sela sing for joy,
let them shout from the tops of the mountains.
Let them give glory to the LORD,
and declare God's praise in the coastlands.

For a long time I have held my peace,
I have kept still and restrained myself;
now I will cry out like a woman in labor,
I will gasp and pant.

I will lay waste mountains and hills,
and dry up all their herbage;
I will turn the rivers into islands,
and dry up the pools.

I will lead the blind
by a road they do not know,
by paths they have not known
I will guide them.

I will turn the darkness before them into light,
the rough places into level ground.
These are the things I will do,
and I will not forsake them.

A time of silence may be observed.

Mark 14:3, 9

While he was at Bethany in the house of Simon
the leper, as he sat at the table, a woman came
with an alabaster jar of very costly ointment of
nard, and she broke open the jar and poured
the ointment on his head. Jesus said, "Truly I
tell you, wherever the good news is proclaimed
in the whole world, what she has done will be
told in remembrance of her."

A time of silence may be observed.

Antiphon for the Song of Mary

By pouring this perfumed oil on Jesus' head,
I am showing my deep love and affection
   for him.
Through me, God is anointing him with oil.

Continue with the Song of Mary, page 54.

TUESDAY

Isaiah 46:3–4

God will carry and will save.

Listen to me, O house of Jacob,
all the remnant of the house of Israel,
who have been borne by me from your birth,
carried from the womb;
even to your old age I am the one,
even when you turn gray I will carry you.

I have made, and I will bear;
I will carry and will save.

A time of silence may be observed.

Luke 7:37–38, 50

And a woman in the city, who was a sinner, having learned that Jesus was eating in the Pharisee's house, brought an alabaster jar of ointment. She stood behind him at his feet, weeping, and began to bathe his feet with her tears and to dry them with her hair. Then she continued kissing his feet and anointing them with the ointment. And he said to the woman, "Your faith has saved you; go in peace."

A time of silence may be observed.

Antiphon for the Song of Mary

I will pour perfumed oil on Jesus' head
to proclaim that he is God's favored one.
Through me, God is anointing him with the oil
    of gladness.

Continue with the Song of Mary, page 54.

WEDNESDAY

Isaiah 66:5–9

Zion was in labor.

Hear the word of the LORD,
you who tremble at God's word:

Your own people who hate you
and reject you for my name's sake
have said, "Let the LORD be glorified,
so that we may see your joy";
but it is they who shall be put to shame.

Listen, an uproar from the city!
A voice from the temple!
The voice of the LORD,
dealing retribution to God's enemies!

Before she was in labor
she gave birth;
before her pain came upon her
she delivered a son.
Who has heard of such a thing?
Who has seen such things?

Shall a land be born in one day?
Shall a nation be delivered in one moment?
Yet as soon as Zion was in labor
she delivered her children.

Shall I open the womb and not deliver?
says the LORD;
shall I, the one who delivers, shut the womb?
says your God.

A time of silence may be observed.

John 12:3, 7–8

Mary took a pound of costly perfume made of pure nard, anointed Jesus' feet, and wiped them with her hair. The house was filled with the fragrance of the perfume. Jesus said, "Leave her alone. She bought it so that she might keep it for the day of my burial. You always have the poor with you, but you do not always have me."

A time of silence may be observed.

Antiphon for the Song of Mary

I am pouring the precious ointment
    on Jesus' head
to affirm that he is a great prophet and leader.
I am confident that God will look on the face
    of the Anointed One.

Continue with the Song of Mary, page 54.

Thursday

Isaiah 66:10–14ab

God will comfort like a mother.

Rejoice with Jerusalem, and be glad for her,
all you who love her;
rejoice with her in joy,
all you who mourn over her—

that you may nurse and be satisfied
from her consoling breast;
that you may drink deeply with delight
from her glorious bosom.

For thus says the LORD:
I will extend prosperity to her like a river,
and the wealth of the nations
like an overflowing stream;
and you shall nurse and be carried on her arm,
and dandled on her knees.

As a mother comforts her child,
so I will comfort you;
you shall be comforted in Jerusalem.

You shall see, and your heart shall rejoice,
your bodies shall flourish like the grass;
and it shall be known that the hand of the LORD
is with God's servants.

A time of silence may be observed.

Matthew 27:55–56

Many women were also there, looking on from a distance; they had followed Jesus from Galilee and had provided for him. Among them were Mary Magdalene, and Mary the mother of James and Joseph, and the mother of the sons of Zebedee.

A time of silence may be observed.

Antiphon for the Song of Mary

When I poured precious nard on Jesus' head,
I proclaimed that he is the Anointed One
   of God.
Through me, God anoints him with the
   precious oil.

Continue with the Song of Mary, page 54.

FRIDAY

Hosea 13:4–6; 14:5–7

God fed Israel in the wilderness.

I have been the LORD your God
ever since the land of Egypt;
you know no God but me,
and besides me there is no savior.

It was I who fed you in the wilderness,
in the land of drought.
When I fed them, they were satisfied;
they were satisfied, and their heart was proud;
therefore they forgot me.

I will be like the dew to Israel;
they shall blossom like the lily,
they shall strike root like the forest of Lebanon.
Their shoots shall spread out;
their beauty shall be like the olive tree,
and their fragrance like that of Lebanon.

They shall again live beneath my shadow,
they shall flourish as a garden;
they shall blossom like the vine,
their fragrance shall be like the wine of Lebanon.

A time of silence may be observed.

Mark 15:40–41

There were also women looking on from a distance; among them were Mary Magdalene, and Mary the mother of James the younger and of Joses, and Salome. These used to follow him and provided for him when he was in Galilee; and there were many other women who had come up with him to Jerusalem.

A time of silence may be observed.

Antiphon for the Song of Mary

I am pouring costly ointment on Jesus' head
to consecrate him as prophet and healer.
I am sure that God will make his face shine.

Continue with the Song of Mary, page 54.

SATURDAY

Deuteronomy 32:10–15, 18

God nurses Israel with honey.

The Most High sustained you in a desert land,
in a howling wilderness waste;
God shielded you, cared for you,
guarded you as the apple of his eye.

As an eagle stirs up its nest,
and hovers over its young;
as it spreads its wings, takes them up,
and bears them aloft on its pinions,
the LORD alone guided you;
no foreign god was with you.

The Most High set you atop the heights
    of the land,
and fed you with produce of the field;
God nursed you with honey from the crags,
with oil from flinty rock;

curds from the herd, and milk from the flock,
with fat of lambs and rams;
Bashan bulls and goats,
together with the choicest wheat—
you drank fine wine from the blood of grapes.

Jacob ate his fill;
Jeshurun grew fat, and kicked.
You grew fat, bloated, and gorged!
You abandoned God who made you,
and scoffed at the Rock of your salvation.

You were unmindful of the Rock that bore you;
you forgot the God who gave you birth.

A time of silence may be observed.

Luke 23:53–56

Then Joseph took Jesus' body down, wrapped it in a linen cloth, and laid it in a rock-hewn tomb where no one had ever been laid. It was the day of Preparation, and the sabbath was beginning. The women who had come with him from Galilee followed, and they saw the tomb and how his body was laid. Then they returned, and prepared spices and ointments. On the sabbath they rested according to the commandment.

A time of silence may be observed.

Antiphon for the Song of Mary

When I poured the precious oil on Jesus' head,
I was preparing his body for burial.
I am sure that God will protect the
    Anointed One.

Continue with the Song of Mary.

SONG OF MARY *Luke 2:47–55*

My soul proclaims the greatness of the Lord,
my spirit rejoices in God my Savior,
for you, Lord, have looked with favor
    on your lowly servant.

From this day all generations will call
  me blessed:
you, the Almighty, have done great things for me
and holy is your name.
You have mercy on those who fear you,
from generation to generation.

You have shown strength with your arm
and scattered the proud in their conceit,
casting down the mighty from their thrones
and lifting up the lowly.
You have filled the hungry with good things
and sent the rich away empty.

You have come to the aid of your servant Israel,
to remember the promise of mercy,
the promise made to our forebears,
to Abraham and his children for ever.

The antiphon is repeated.

INTERCESSIONS

Response to each invocation:
    Lord, have mercy.

That all know God's love on their journey:
That we hear God's challenging word:
That we honor the dignity of each person:
That we lend our voices to the prophets:
That we grow impatient with injustice:

That we know delight in one another:
That prisoners not be forgotten:
That the old not be forgotten:
That those who confront oppression
    be strengthened:
That those who challenge deception
    be strengthened:
That all the world know the joy of God's love:

LORD'S PRAYER

CLOSING PRAYER

God of the covenant,
our days end
and often we have wandered from you.
In the evening darkness call to us,
and with rejoicing
we shall rest again in your arms,
welcomed, made whole, anointed.
We pray in the name of Jesus,
the Christ, the Anointed One,
the Lord for ever and ever.
~*Amen.*

BLESSING

May the compassionate and merciful God
give us a restful night
and peace at the last.
~*Amen.*

SIGN OF PEACE

WOMEN EVANGELISTS AND APOSTLES

The canticles of Morning Prayer are songs of women leaders and prophets of the Hebrew scriptures, foremothers of the women evangelists and apostles of the church. The readings speak of Jesus' ministry among women. These women are considered to be evangelists inasmuch as they told others about Jesus and what he had done for them. The antiphons for the Song of Hannah are from psalms and contain maternal and other feminine images of God.

At Evening Prayer, the psalms also contain such maternal and other feminine images of God. The psalms for Friday and Saturday are taken from the Common of Apostles of the Roman Catholic Liturgy of the Hours. The readings all tell of women of the early church, mostly leaders. Many of the antiphons for the Song of Mary are based on John 15:15–17.

MORNING PRAYER

If a preparation rite is used, this verse is spoken or chanted:
> Give thanks!
> Many believed in Jesus because of the
> woman's testimony.

OPENING VERSE

> I have called you friends
> because I have shared everything with you.
> You did not choose me, but I chose you,
> and I appointed you to go and bear fruit.

SONG

> Awake with timbrel and with dance,
> and sing to God on high.
> With olive wreath and waving branch
> our Maker magnify!
>
> Join Sarah, blest with laughing child,
> and Deborah, fierce and strong.
> Join Judith's spirit, undefiled,
> and Miriam's triumph song.
>
> Hear Christ call "Little girl, arise!"
> as Jairus' daughter lives.
> Watch bent grow straight, and recognize
> the healing Jesus gives.

Awake with song and glad acclaim.
God's daily gifts discern.
With Martha, name Christ's holy name.
With Mary, seek and learn.

CM (86.86)

MORNING THANKSGIVING

O God, you are the source of everything good.
~Accept our morning thanks and praise.

We give you thanks for our mothers in faith,
for Sarah and Hagar, Rebekah, Rachel
    and Leah,
for the prophets Miriam and Deborah,
for Judith and Esther, the saviors of their people.
~Accept our morning thanks and praise.

We give you thanks for Jesus,
who sent women to tell the gospel:
Mary Magdalene, Martha and Mary,
the woman of Samaria.
~Accept our morning thanks and praise.

We give you thanks for the Holy Spirit,
bold Spirit who bids us proclaim
the gospel of justice and of peace.
~Accept our morning thanks and praise.

FIRST PSALM/CANTICLE

Psalm 117

Strong is God's love for us.

Alleluia!

O praise the LORD, all you nations,
acclaim God all you peoples!

Strong is God's love for us;
the LORD is faithful for ever.

A time of silence may be observed.

SECOND PSALM/CANTICLE, READING AND ANTIPHON

The second psalm/canticle, the reading and the antiphon for the Song of Hannah are arranged according to the days of the week.

SUNDAY

Genesis 17:15–16, 21

Sarah shall give rise to nations.

God said to Abraham,
"As for Sarah your wife,
you shall not call her Sarai,
but Sarah shall be her name.

"I will bless her,
and moreover I will give you a son by her.

"I will bless her,
and she shall give rise to nations;
kings of peoples shall come from her.

"My covenant I will establish with Isaac,
whom Sarah shall bear to you at this season
next year."

A time of silence may be observed.

Mark 5:22–23, 41–42a

Then one of the leaders of the synagogue named
Jairus came and, when he saw Jesus, fell at his
feet and begged him repeatedly, "My little
daughter is at the point of death. Come and lay
your hands on her, so that she may be made
well, and live." Jesus took her by the hand and
said to her, "Talitha cum," which means, "Little
girl, get up!" And immediately the girl got
up and began to walk about (she was twelve
years of age).

A time of silence may be observed.

Antiphon for the Song of Hannah

Display your great love,
you whose right hand saves your friends
    from those who rebel against them.
In my justice I shall see your face
and be filled, when I awake,
    with the sight of your glory.

Continue with the Song of Hannah, page 74.

MONDAY

Exodus 15:19–21

Sing to the LORD, who has triumphed gloriously.

When the horses of Pharoah
with his chariots and his chariot drivers went
    into the sea,
the LORD brought back the waters of the sea
    upon them;
but the Israelites walked through the sea
    on dry ground.

Then the prophet Miriam, Aaron's sister,
took a tambourine in her hand;
and all the women went out after her
with tambourines and with dancing.

And Miriam sang to them:
"Sing to the LORD,
for God has triumphed gloriously;
horse and rider God has thrown into the sea."

A time of silence may be observed.

John 4:28–29, 39

Then the woman left her water jar and went
back to the city. She said to the people, "Come
and see a man who told me everything I have
ever done! He cannot be the Messiah, can he?"
Many Samaritans from that city believed in
Jesus because of the woman's testimony,
"He told me everything I have ever done."

A time of silence may be observed.

Antiphon for the Song of Hannah

Keep a loving eye on me;
guard me under your wings.
Hide me from those who attack,
from predators who surround me.

Continue with the Song of Hannah, page 74.

TUESDAY

Judges 5:3–4, 7–9

Deborah arose as a mother in Israel.

Hear, O kings; give ear, O princes;
to the LORD I will sing,
I will make melody to the LORD,
    the God of Israel.

LORD, when you sent out from Seir,
when you marched from the region of Edom,
the earth trembled,
and the heavens poured,
the clouds indeed poured water.

The peasantry prospered in Israel,
they grew fat on plunder,
because you arose, Deborah,
arose as a mother in Israel.

When new gods were chosen,
then war was in the gates.
Was shield or spear to be seen
among forty thousand in Israel?

My heart goes out to the commanders of Israel
who offered themselves willingly
    among the people.
Bless the LORD.

A time of silence may be observed.

Luke 4:38–39

After leaving the synagogue Jesus entered
Simon's house. Now Simon's mother-in-law
was suffering from a high fever, and they asked
him about her. Then he stood over her and
rebuked the fever, and it left her. Immediately
she got up and began to serve them.

A time of silence may be observed.

Antiphon for the Song of Hannah

Shadow me with your wings
until all danger passes.
Extend to me, O God,
your love that never fails.

Continue with the Song of Hannah, page 74.

WEDNESDAY

Judges 5:10–12a

Tell, O Deborah, the triumphs of the LORD.

Tell of it, you who ride on white donkeys,
you who sit on rich carpets
and you who walk by the way.

To the sound of musicians
  at the watering places,
there they repeat the triumphs of the LORD,
the triumphs of his peasantry in Israel.

Then down to the gates marched the people
  of the Lord.
Awake, awake, Deborah!
Awake, awake, utter a song!

A time of silence may be observed.

John 11:25–27

Jesus said to Martha, "I am the resurrection and
the life. Those who believe in me, even though
they die, will live, and everyone who lives and
believes in me will never die. Do you believe
this?" She said to him, "Yes, Lord, I believe that
you are the Messiah, the Son of God, the one
coming into the world."

A time of silence may be observed.

Antiphon for the Song of Hannah

I will proclaim your name to my people,
I will praise you in the assembly.
In you our forebears put their trust;
they trusted and you set them free.

Continue with the Song of Hannah, page 74.

THURSDAY

Judith 13:18a, 19–20

Blessed are you, O Judith.

Then Uzziah said to Judith,
"O daughter, you are blessed
   by the Most High God
above all other women on earth;
and blessed be the Lord God,
who created the heavens and the earth.

"Your praise will never depart
from the hearts of those
who remember the power of God.

"May God grant this to be a perpetual honor
   to you,
and may God reward you with blessings,
because you risked your own life
when our nation was brought low,
and you averted our ruin,
walking in the straight path before our God."

And all the people said, "Amen. Amen."

A time of silence may be observed.

Luke 13:11–13

And just then there appeared a woman with
a spirit that had crippled her for eighteen years.
She was bent over and was quite unable to
stand up straight. When Jesus saw her, he called
her over and said, "Woman, you are set free
from your ailment." When he laid his hands
on her, immediately she stood up straight and
began praising God.

A time of silence may be observed.

Antiphon for the Song of Hannah

Welcome me into your home,
under your wings for ever.
Give me the blessings
of those who honor your name.

Continue with the Song of Hannah, page 74.

FRIDAY

Judith 15:14—16:5

By the hand of a woman God triumphs.

Judith began this thanksgiving before all Israel,
and all the people loudly sang this song of praise.

And Judith said,
"Begin a song to my God with tambourines,
sing to my Lord with cymbals.

"Raise to God a new psalm;
exalt and call upon God's name.

"For the Lord is a God who crushes wars
and sets up camp among the chosen people;
God delivered me from the hands
    of my pursuers.

"The Assyrians came down from the mountains
    of the north;
they came with myriads of warriors;
their numbers blocked up the wadis,
and their cavalry covered the hills.

"They boasted that they would burn up
    my territory,
and kill my youth with the sword,
and dash my infants to the ground,
and seize my children as booty,
and take my virgins as spoil.

"But the Lord Almighty has foiled them
by the hand of a woman."

A time of silence may be observed.

Mark 7:25–26, 30

A woman whose little daughter had an unclean spirit immediately heard about Jesus, and she came and bowed down at his feet. Now the woman was a Gentile, of Syrophoenician origin. She begged him to cast the demon out of her daughter. She went home, found the child lying on the bed, and the demon gone.

A time of silence may be observed.

Antiphon for the Song of Hannah

You love those centered in truth;
teach me your hidden wisdom.
Wash me with fresh water;
wash me bright as snow.

Continue with the Song of Hannah, page 74.

SATURDAY

Judith 15:14; 16:6–10, 13

The Lord is wonderful in strength.

Judith began this thanksgiving before all Israel, and all the people loudly sang this song of praise.

"Their mighty one did not fall by the hands of
   the young men,
nor did the sons of the Titans strike him down,
nor did tall giants set upon him;
but Judith daughter of Merari
with the beauty of her countenance undid him.

"For she put away her widow's clothing
to exalt the oppressed in Israel.
She anointed her face with perfume;
she fastened her hair with a tiara
and put on a linen gown to beguile him.

"Her sandal ravished his eyes,
her beauty captivated his mind,
and the sword severed his neck!
The Persians trembled at her boldness,
the Medes were daunted at her daring.

"I will sing to my God a new song.
O Lord, you are great and glorious,
wonderful in strength, invincible."

A time of silence may be observed.

Matthew 9:20–22

Then suddenly a woman who had been suffering
from hemorrhages for twelve years came up
behind him and touched the fringe of his cloak,
for she said to herself, "If I only touch his cloak,

I will be made well." Jesus turned, and seeing her he said, "Take heart, daughter; your faith has made you well." And instantly the woman was made well.

A time of silence may be observed.

Antiphon for the Song of Hannah

God befriends the faithful,
teaches them the covenant,
God's ways are faithful love
for those who keep the covenant.

Continue with the Song of Hannah.

SONG OF HANNAH *1 Samuel 2:1b–2, 5, 7–9*

My heart exults in the LORD,
my strength is exalted in my God.
My mouth derides my enemies,
because I rejoice in my victory.

There is no Holy One like the LORD,
no one besides you;
there is no Rock like our God.

Those who were full have hired themselves out
  for bread,
but those who were hungry are fat with spoil.
The barren has borne seven,
but she who has many children is forlorn.

The LORD makes poor and makes rich;
God brings low but also exalts.
The Most High raises up the poor from the dust,
lifts the needy from the ash heap,
to make them sit with princes
and inherit a seat of honor.

For the pillars of the earth are the LORD's,
and on them God has set the world.
The Most High will guard the feet
  of the faithful ones,
but the wicked shall be cut off in darkness;
for not by might does one prevail.

The antiphon is repeated.

LITANY OF PRAISE

Response to each invocation:
  May we proclaim the gospel.

  Christ, living water:
  Christ, compassionate guest:
  Christ, dearest friend:
  Christ, teacher and learner:

Christ, fullness of life:
Christ, friend to women and men alike:
Christ, protector of the young:
Christ, giving dignity to the elderly:
Christ, seeking out the stranger:
Christ, surrounding us with blessing:

LORD'S PRAYER

CLOSING PRAYER

Raise us up, God of our ancestors,
as you once raised up for your people
women and men who proclaimed,
some in word and some in deed,
that you alone are God
and that to you belong
all our heart, all our soul, all our might.
We pray in Jesus' name,
who is Lord for ever and ever.
~*Amen.*

BLESSING

Let us bless the Lord.
~*Thanks be to God.*

SIGN OF PEACE

EVENING PRAYER

If a preparation rite is used, this verse is spoken or chanted:
Rejoice!
Jesus Christ is the light of the world:
A light no darkness can extinguish.

OPENING VERSE

Guard me as the apple of your eye;
hide me in the shadow of your wings.
Let us dwell in the shelter of the Most High
and abide in the shadow of the Almighty.

SONG

To call the names of faithful ones
who labored side by side
to share the gospel of our Christ,
we join at eventide:

For Rufus' mother, dear to Paul,
and Prisca, whom he prized,
for Lydia, who led the way,
her household all baptized.

For Tabitha, raised from the dead,
restored to friends who grieved,
Euodia and Syntyche,
Damaris who believed.

For Junia and Nympha, too,
and hundreds now unknown,
we join in grateful praise and prayer
to make their faith our own.

CM (86.86)

EVENING THANKSGIVING

Blessed are you, O God, vigilant mother.
~*Blessed are you, O God.*

From the beginning you have rejoiced
    in creation,
dancing with us in joy and in tears,
guarding us as the apple of your eye.
~*Blessed are you, O God.*

In the course of time you gave us Jesus,
who has ever raised up women and men
to spread the good news of your justice.
~*Blessed are you, O God.*

Today we are sent by your Spirit,
    guardian of the poor,
to nurture and care, to proclaim and rejoice.
~*Blessed are you, O God.*

FIRST PSALM/CANTICLE

Psalm 150

Sing praise.

Alleluia!

Praise God in the holy place,
sing praise in the mighty heavens.
Sing praise for God's powerful deeds,
praise God's surpassing greatness.

Sing praise with sound of trumpet,
sing praise with lute and harp.
Sing praise with timbrel and dance,
sing praise with strings and pipes.

Sing praise with resounding cymbals,
sing praise with clashing of cymbals.
Let everything that lives and that breathes
give praise to the LORD. Alleluia!

A time of silence may be observed.

SECOND PSALM/CANTICLE, READING AND ANTIPHON

The second psalm/canticle, the reading and the antiphon for the Song of Mary are arranged according to the days of the week.

SUNDAY

Psalm 17:6–15

Hide me in the shadow of your wings.

I am here and I call; you will hear me, O God.
Turn your ear to me; hear my words.
Display your great love,
you whose right hand saves your friends
from those who rebel against them.

Guard me as the apple of your eye.
Hide me in the shadow of your wings
from the violent attack of the wicked.

My foes encircle me with deadly intent.
Their hearts tight shut, their mouths
    speak proudly.
They advance against me, and now they
    surround me.

Their eyes are watching to strike me
   to the ground,
as though they were lions ready to claw
or like some young lion crouched in hiding.

LORD, arise, confront them, strike them down!
Let your sword rescue me from the wicked;
let your hand, O LORD, rescue me,
from those whose reward is in this present life.

You give them their fill of your treasures;
they rejoice in abundance of offspring
and leave their wealth to their children.

As for me, in my justice I shall see your face
and be filled, when I awake, with the sight
   of your glory.

A time of silence may be observed.

Acts of the Apostles 9:36–37, 40

Now in Joppa there was a disciple whose name
was Tabitha, which in Greek is Dorcas. She was
devoted to good works and acts of charity. At
that time she became ill and died. When they
had washed her, they laid her in a room upstairs.
Peter put all of them outside, and then he knelt
down and prayed. He turned to the body and

said, "Tabitha, get up." Then she opened her
eyes, and seeing Peter, she sat up.

A time of silence may be observed.

Antiphon for the Song of Mary

You are my friends,
for you have remained steadfast in my love.

Continue with the Song of Mary, page 94.

MONDAY

Psalm 57:2–6

In the shadow of your wings I will take refuge.

Have mercy on me, God, have mercy,
for in you my soul has taken refuge.
In the shadow of your wings I take refuge
till the storms of destruction pass by.

I call to you God the Most High,
to you who have always been my help.
May you send from heaven and save me
and shame those who assail me.

O God, send your truth and your love.

My soul lies down among lions,
who would devour us, one and all.
Their teeth are spears and arrows,
their tongue a sharpened sword.

O God, arise above the heavens;
may your glory shine on earth!

A time of silence may be observed.

Acts of the Apostles 16:13–15

On the sabbath day we went outside the gate
by the river, where we supposed there was a
place of prayer; and we sat down and spoke to
the women who had gathered there. A certain
woman named Lydia, a worshiper of God,
was listening to us; she was from the city of
Thyatira and a dealer in purple cloth. The Lord
opened her heart to listen eagerly to what was
said by Paul. When she and her household were
baptized, she urged us, saying, "If you have
judged me to be faithful to the Lord, come and
stay at my home." And she prevailed upon us.

A time of silence may be observed.

Antiphon for the Song of Mary

You did not choose me,
but I chose you to go forth
and bear fruit that will last for ever.

Continue with the Song of Mary, page 94.

TUESDAY

Psalm 22:4–6, 10–12, 23–32

It was God who took me from the womb.

Yet you, O God, are holy,
enthroned on the praises of Israel.
In you our forebears put their trust;
they trusted and you set them free.
When they cried to you, they escaped.
In you they trusted and never in vain.

Yes, it was you who took me from the womb,
entrusted me to my mother's breast.
To you I was committed from my birth,
from my mother's womb you have been
    my God.
Do not leave me alone in my distress;
come close, there is none else to help.

I will tell of your name to my people
and praise you where they are assembled.
"You who fear the LORD give praise;
all children of Jacob, give glory.
Revere God, children of Israel.

"For God has never despised
nor scorned the poverty of the poor,
nor looked away from them,
but has heard the poor when they cried."

You are my praise in the great assembly.
My vows I will pay before those who fear God.
The poor shall eat and shall have their fill.
Those who seek the LORD shall praise the LORD.
May their hearts live for ever and ever!

All the earth shall remember and return
    to the LORD,
all families of the nations shall bow down in awe;
for the kingdom is the LORD's,
    who is ruler of all.
They shall bow down in awe, all the mighty
    of the earth,
all who must die and go down to the dust.

My soul shall live for God and my children too
    shall serve.
They shall tell of the Lord to generations yet
    to come;
declare to those unborn the faithfulness of God.
"These things the Lord has done."

A time of silence may be observed.

Acts of the Apostles 17:2, 4, 34

Paul went in, as was his custom, and on three
sabbath days argued with the Thessalonians from
the scriptures. Some of them were persuaded
and joined Paul and Silas, as did a great many
of the devout Greeks and not a few of the
leading women. Some of the Athenians joined
him and became believers, including Dionysius
the Areopagite and a woman named Damaris,
and others with them.

A time of silence may be observed.

Antiphon for the Song of Mary

This I ask: that you love each other
as I have loved you.
I look on you as friends.

Continue with the Song of Mary, page 94.

WEDNESDAY

Psalm 61

*Let me find refuge under the shelter
of your wings.*

O God, hear my cry!
Listen to my prayer!
From the end of the earth I call;
my heart is faint.

On a rock too high for me to reach
set me on high.
O you who have been my refuge,
my tower against the foe.

Let me dwell in your tent for ever
and hide in the shelter of your wings.
For you, O God, hear my prayer,
grant me the heritage of those who fear you.

May you lengthen the life of the king;
may his years cover many generations.
May he ever sit enthroned before God;
bid love and truth be his protection.

So I will always praise your name
and day after day fulfill my vows.

A time of silence may be observed.

Romans 16:1–3

I commend to you our sister Phoebe, a deacon of the church at Cenchreae, so that you may welcome her in the Lord as is fitting for the saints, and help her in whatever she may require from you, for she has been a benefactor of many and of myself as well. Greet Prisca and Aquila, who work with me in Christ Jesus.

A time of silence may be observed.

Antiphon for the Song of Mary

Do not be distressed.
Let your hearts be free,
for I leave with you my peace, my word.

Continue with the Song of Mary, page 94.

THURSDAY

Psalm 91

Under God's wings you will find refuge.

Those who dwell in the shelter
    of the Most High
and abide in the shade of the Almighty
say to the LORD: "My refuge,
my stronghold, my God in whom I trust!"

It is God who will free you from the snare
of the fowler who seeks to destroy you;
God will conceal you with pinions,
and under God's wings you will find refuge.

You will not fear the terror of the night
nor the arrow that flies by day,
nor the plague that prowls in the darkness
nor the scourge that lays waste at noon.

A thousand may fall at your side,
ten thousand fall at your right,
you, it will never approach;
God's faithfulness is buckler and shield.

Your eyes have only to look
to see how the wicked are repaid,
you who have said: "LORD, my refuge!"
And have made the Most High your dwelling.

Upon you no evil shall fall,
no plague approach where you dwell.
For you God has commanded the angels,
to keep you in all your ways.

They shall bear you upon their hands
lest you strike your foot against a stone.
On the lion and the viper you will tread
and trample the young lion and the dragon.

You set your love on me so I will save you,
protect you for you know my name.
When you call I shall answer: "I am with you,"
I will save you in distress and give you glory.

With length of days I will content you;
I shall let you see my saving power.

A time of silence may be observed.

Romans 16:6–7, 12–13

Greet Mary, who has worked very hard among
you. Greet Andronicus and Junia, my relatives
who were in prison with me; they are prominent
among the apostles, and they were in Christ
before I was. Greet those workers in the Lord,
Tryphaena and Tryphosa. Greet the beloved
Persis, who has worked hard in the Lord.
Greet Rufus, chosen in the Lord; and greet
his mother—a mother to me also.

A time of silence may be observed.

Antiphon for the Song of Mary

Their voice has gone out to the limits of the earth,
their words to the ends of the world.

Continue with the Song of Mary, page 94.

FRIDAY

Psalm 116:1–2, 12–19

I bring a gift of thanks.

Alleluia!

I love the LORD, for the LORD has heard
the cry of my appeal.
The LORD was attentive to me
in the day when I called.

How can I repay the LORD
for God's goodness to me?
The cup of salvation I will raise;
I will call on the LORD's name.

My vows to the LORD I will fulfill
before all the people.
O precious in the eyes of the LORD
is the death of the faithful.

Your servant, LORD, your servant am I;
you have loosened my bonds.
A thanksgiving sacrifice I make;
I will call on the LORD's name.

My vows to the LORD I will fulfill
before all the people,
in the courts of the house of the LORD,
in your midst, O Jerusalem.

A time of silence may be observed.

Philippians 4:1–3

Therefore, my brothers and sisters, whom
I love and long for, my joy and crown, stand
firm in the Lord in this way, my beloved. I urge
Euodia and I urge Syntyche to be of the same
mind in the Lord. Yes, and I ask you also, my
loyal companions, help these women, for they
have struggled beside me in the work of the
gospel, together with Clement and the rest of
my coworkers, whose names are in the book
of life.

A time of silence may be observed.

Antiphon for the Song of Mary

They proclaimed what God has done for us.
They grasped the meaning of God's deeds.

Continue with the Song of Mary, page 94.

SATURDAY

Psalm 126

They hold high the harvest.

When the LORD delivered Zion from bondage,
it seemed like a dream.
Then was our mouth filled with laughter,
on our lips there were songs.

The heathens themselves said:
"What marvels the LORD worked for them!"
What marvels the LORD worked for us!
Indeed we were glad.

Deliver us, O LORD, from our bondage
as streams in dry land.
Those who are sowing in tears
will sing when they reap.

They go out, they go out, full of tears,
carrying seed for the sowing;
they come back, they come back, full of song,
carrying their sheaves.

A time of silence may be observed.

Colossians 4:15–18

Give my greetings to the brothers and sisters
in Laodicea, and to Nympha and the church in
her house. And when this letter has been read
among you, have it read also in the church of the
Laodiceans; and see that you read also the letter
from Laodicea. And say to Archippus, "See that
you complete the task that you have received
in the Lord." I, Paul, write this greeting with
my own hand. Remember my chains. Grace be
with you.

A time of silence may be observed.

Antiphon for the Song of Mary

You are my friends
if you are faithful to my words.
You are fellow citizens of the saints
and members of the household of God.

Continue with the Song of Mary.

SONG OF MARY *Luke 2:47–55*

My soul proclaims the greatness of the Lord,
my spirit rejoices in God my Savior,
for you, Lord, have looked with favor
  on your lowly servant.

From this day all generations will call
   me blessed:
you, the Almighty, have done great things for me
and holy is your name.
You have mercy on those who fear you,
from generation to generation.

You have shown strength with your arm
and scattered the proud in their conceit,
casting down the mighty from their thrones
and lifting up the lowly.
You have filled the hungry with good things
and sent the rich away empty.

You have come to the aid of your servant Israel,
to remember the promise of mercy,
the promise made to our forebears,
to Abraham and his children for ever.

The antiphon is repeated.

INTERCESSIONS

Response to each invocation:
   Lord, have mercy.

That we listen to the poor and oppressed:
That we ponder more and more the words
   of scripture:
That artists of word and music bring
   forth beauty:

That artists of dance and image bring
   forth beauty:
That builders and artisans bring forth beauty:
That athletes and scholars bring forth beauty:
That those who serve the law work for justice:
That those who seek power also seek wisdom:
That we may live in harmony with the earth:
That we may live in harmony with one another:
That children have nothing to fear:
That the old have nothing to fear:
That those with disabilities have nothing to fear:

LORD'S PRAYER

CLOSING PRAYER

At the day's end we come home to you, O God,
with much or little to show for this day
lived in the light of your gospel.
Give us shelter and refresh us with your love
that we might give as freely as we have received.
We pray in Jesus' name,
who is Lord for ever and ever.
~*Amen.*

BLESSING

May the compassionate and merciful God
give us a restful night
and peace at the last.
~*Amen.*

SIGN OF PEACE

HOLY WISDOM

At Morning Prayer, the canticles speak of Holy Wisdom and thank God for her. Passages from the scriptures are used that give examples of wisdom in speech or action. The antiphons for the Song of Hannah are taken from the hymn to Wisdom in chapter 24 of the book of Sirach.

At Evening Prayer also, the canticles speak of Holy Wisdom and thank God for her. Passages from the Christian scriptures are used that give examples of wisdom. The antiphons for the Song of Mary are taken from the beatitudes in chapter five of Matthew's gospel, understood as examples of wisdom.

MORNING PRAYER

If a preparation rite is used, this verse is spoken or chanted:
> Give thanks!
> Before the ages, in the beginning,
>   God created me,
> and for all the ages I shall not cease to be.

OPENING VERSE

> Happy are those who find wisdom
> and those who get understanding.
> She is a tree of life to those who lay hold of her;
> those who hold her fast are called happy.

SONG

> Through silver veils of morning mist
> break rays of golden sun.
> In amethyst and ruby skies,
> a new day has begun.
>
> More treasured yet than silver, gold,
> or any precious gem,
> God's Wisdom breaks upon the earth
> and wakes our morning hymn.
>
> A radiant and unfading light
> now shines before our eyes,
> with insight for all minds that seek
> and truth to make us wise.

Sophia calls us to the feast
of wine and living bread,
where fruits of grace and peace abound
and hungry hearts are fed.

With Huldah, Hannah, Miriam,
and womenfolk unnamed,
we cherish our inheritance
of prophecy proclaimed:

The needy shall be lifted up.
The weak shall be made strong.
And Wisdom's flow'ring tree of life
shall blossom in our song.

CM (86.86)

MORNING THANKSGIVING

✓ O God, you are the source of all wisdom.
  ~Accept our morning thanks and praise.

We give you thanks for the wisdom
    of your Torah, your law,
which invites us to love you with all our heart
and all our soul and all our might.
~Accept our morning thanks and praise.

We give you thanks for Jesus,
Wisdom herself made flesh to dwell among us,
who calls all alike to your table.
~Accept our morning thanks and praise.

We give you thanks for the Holy Spirit,
Wisdom creating and reviving,
in whom we live and move and have our being.
~*Accept our morning thanks and praise.* ✓

FIRST PSALM/CANTICLE

Sirach 24:1–12

Wisdom tells of her glory.

Wisdom praises herself,
and tells of her glory in the midst of her people.
In the assembly of the Most High she opens
    her mouth,
and in the presence of God's hosts she tells
    of her glory:

"I came forth from the mouth of the Most High,
and covered the earth like a mist.
I dwelt in the highest heavens,
and my throne was in a pillar of cloud.

"Alone I compassed the vault of heaven
and traversed the depths of the abyss.
Over waves of the sea, over all the earth,
and over every people and nation I have
    held sway.

"Among all these I sought a resting place;
in whose territory should I abide?
Then the Creator of all things gave me
   a command,
and my Creator chose the place for my tent.

"God said, 'Make your dwelling in Jacob,
and in Israel receive your inheritance.'
Before the ages, in the beginning,
   God created me,
and for all the ages I shall not cease to be.

"In the holy tent I ministered
   before the Most High,
and so I was established in Zion.
Thus in the beloved city God gave me
   a resting place,
and in Jerusalem was my domain.

"I took root in an honored people,
in the portion of the Lord, God's heritage."

A time of silence may be observed.

SECOND PSALM/CANTICLE, READING AND ANTIPHON

The second psalm/canticle, the reading and the antiphon for the Song of Hannah are arranged according to the days of the week.

SUNDAY

Proverbs 3:13–18

Wisdom is a tree of life.

Happy are those who find wisdom,
and those who get understanding,
for her income is better than silver,
and her revenue better than gold.

She is more precious than jewels,
and nothing you desire can compare with her.
Long life is in her right hand;
in her left hand are riches and honor.

Her ways are ways of pleasantness,
and all her paths are peace.
She is a tree of life to those who lay hold of her,
those who hold her fast are called happy.

A time of silence may be observed.

Deuteronomy 6:4–7

Hear, O Israel: The LORD is our God, the LORD alone. You shall love the LORD your God with all your heart, and with all your soul, and with all your might. Keep these words that I am commanding you today in your heart. Recite them to your children and talk about them when you are at home and when you are away, when you lie down and when you rise.

A time of silence may be observed.

Antiphon for the Song of Hannah

Wisdom grew tall like a cedar in Lebanon,
and like a cypress on the heights of Hermon.

Continue with the Song of Hannah, page 117.

MONDAY

Proverbs 4:5–13

Prize wisdom highly.

Get wisdom; get insight: do not forget,
   nor turn away
from the words of my mouth.

Do not forsake her, and she will keep you;
love her, and she will guard you.

The beginning of wisdom is this: Get wisdom,
and whatever else you get, get insight.

Prize her highly, and she will exalt you;
she will honor you if you embrace her.

She will place on your head a fair garland;
she will bestow on you a beautiful crown.

Hear my child, and accept my words,
that the years of your life may be many.

I have taught you the way of wisdom;
I have led you in the paths of uprightness.

When you walk, your step will not
   be hampered;
and if you run, you will not stumble.

Keep hold to instruction; do not let go;
guard her, for she is your life.

A time of silence may be observed.

2 Kings 22:13–14

King Josiah said to his servants, "Go, inquire of
the LORD for me, for the people, and for all
Judah, concerning the words of this book that

has been found; for great is the wrath of the
LORD that is kindled against us, because
our ancestors did not obey the words of this
book, to do according to all that is written
concerning us." So the priest Hilkiah, Ahikam,
Achbor, Shaphan, and Asaiah went to the
prophetess Huldah the wife of Shallum son of
Tikvah, son of Harhas, keeper of the wardrobe;
she resided in Jerusalem in the Second Quarter,
where they consulted her.

A time of silence may be observed.

Antiphon for the Song of Hannah

Wisdom grew tall like a palm tree in En-gedi,
and like rosebushes in Jericho.

Continue with the Song of Hannah, page 117.

TUESDAY

Proverbs 8:1–11

Does not wisdom call?

Does not wisdom call,
and does not understanding raise her voice?

On the heights, beside the way,
at the crossroads she takes her stand;
beside the gates in front of the town,
at the entrance of the portals she cries out:

"To you, O people, I call,
and my cry is to all that live.
O simple ones, learn prudence;
acquire intelligence, you who lack it.

"Hear, for I will speak noble things,
and from my lips will come what is right;
for my mouth will utter truth;
wickedness is an abomination to my lips.

"All the words of my mouth are righteous;
there is nothing twisted or crooked in them.
They are all straight to one who understands
and right to those who find knowledge.

"Take my instructions instead of silver,
and knowledge rather than choice gold;
for wisdom is better than jewels,
and all that you may desire cannot compare
    with her."

A time of silence may be observed.

2 Kings 5:1–3

Naaman, commander of the army of the king of Aram, was a great man and in high favor with his master, because by him the LORD had given victory to Aram. The man, though a mighty warrior, suffered from leprosy. Now the Arameans on one of their raids had taken a young girl captive from the land of Israel, and she served Naaman's wife. She said to her mistress, "If only my lord were with the prophet who is in Samaria! He would cure him of his leprosy."

A time of silence may be observed.

Antiphon for the Song of Hannah

Wisdom grew tall like a fair olive tree in the field, and like a plane tree beside water.

Continue with the Song of Hannah, page 117.

WEDNESDAY

Proverbs 8:12–21

Wisdom is better than jewels.

I, wisdom, live with prudence,
and I attain knowledge and discretion.

The fear of the LORD is hatred of evil.
Pride and arrogance and the way of evil
and perverted speech I hate.

I have good advice and sound wisdom;
I have insight, I have strength.

By me kings reign,
and rulers decree what is just;
by me rulers rule,
and nobles, all who govern rightly.

I love those who love me,
and those who seek me diligently find me.

Riches and honor are with me,
enduring wealth and prosperity.
My fruit is better than gold, even fine gold,
and my yield than choice silver.

I walk in the way of righteousness,
along the paths of justice,
endowing with wealth those who love me
and filling their treasuries.

A time of silence may be observed.

Numbers 27:1a, 2, 4

Then the daughters of Zelophehad came
forward. They stood before Moses, Eleazar
the priest, the leaders, and all the congregation,

at the entrance of the tent of meeting, and
they said, "Why should the name of our father
be taken away from his clan because he had
no son? Give to us a possession among our
father's brothers."

A time of silence may be observed.

Antiphon for the Song of Hannah

Like a terebinth wisdom spread out
   her branches,
and her branches are glorious and graceful.

Continue with the Song of Hannah, page 117.

THURSDAY

Proverbs 9:1–6, 10–11

Wisdom has set her table.

Wisdom has built her house,
she has hewn her seven pillars.

She has slaughtered her animals,
she has mixed her wine,
she has also set her table.
She has sent out her servant-girls, she calls
from the highest places in the town,

"You that are simple, turn in here!"
To those without sense she says,
"Come, eat of my bread
and drink of the wine I have mixed.
Lay aside immaturity, and live,
and walk in the way of insight."

The fear of the LORD is the beginning of wisdom,
and the knowledge of the Holy One is insight.

For by me your days will be multiplied,
and years will be added to your life.

A time of silence may be observed.

2 Kings 4:8–10

One day Elisha was passing through Shunem,
where a wealthy woman lived, who urged him
to have a meal. So whenever he passed that way,
he would stop there for a meal. She said to her
husband, "Look, I am sure that this man who
regularly passes our way is a holy man of God.
Let us make a small roof chamber with walls,
and put there for him a bed, a table, a chair, and
a lamp, so that he can stay there whenever he
comes to us."

A time of silence may be observed.

Antiphon for the Song of Hannah

Like the vine wisdom buds forth delights,
and her blossoms become glorious and
abundant fruit.

Continue with the Song of Hannah, page 117.

FRIDAY

Wisdom of Solomon 6:12–16

Wisdom is radiant and unfading.

Wisdom is radiant and unfading,
and she is easily discerned by those who love her,
and is found by those who seek her.

She hastens to make herself known to those
who desire her.
One who rises early to see her will have
no difficulty,
for she will be found sitting at the gate.

To fix one's thought on her is
   perfect understanding,
and one who is vigilant on her account
   will soon be free from care,
because she goes about seeking those worthy
   of her,
and she graciously appears to them
   in their paths,
and meets them in every thought.

A time of silence may be observed.

Exodus 1:15–19

The king of Egypt said to the Hebrew midwives,
one of whom was named Shiphrah and the
other Puah, "When you act as midwives to the
Hebrew women, and see them on the birth-
stool, if it is a boy, kill him; but if it is a girl, she
shall live." But the midwives feared God; they
did not do as the king of Egypt commanded
them, but they let the boys live. So the king of
Egypt summoned the midwives and said to
them, "Why have you done this, and allowed
the boys to live?" The midwives said to Pharoah,
"Because the Hebrew women are not like the
Egyptian women; for they are vigorous and give
birth before the midwife comes to them."

A time of silence may be observed.

Antiphon for the Song of Hannah

The memory of wisdom is sweeter than honey,
and the possession of wisdom sweeter than
    the honeycomb.

Continue with the Song of Hannah, page 117.

SATURDAY

Wisdom of Solomon 7:7–14

Wisdom's radiance never ceases.

I prayed, and understanding was given me;
I called on God, and the spirit of wisdom came
    to me.
I preferred her to scepters and thrones,
and I accounted wealth as nothing
    in comparison with her.

Neither did I liken to her any priceless gem,
because all gold is but a little sand in her sight,
and silver will be accounted as clay before her.
I loved her more than health and beauty,
and I chose to have her rather than light,
because her radiance never ceases.

All good things came to me along with her,
and in her hands uncounted wealth.

I rejoiced in them all, because wisdom
    leads them;
but I did not know that she was their mother.

I learned without guile and I impart
    without grudging;
I do not hide her wealth.

For it is an unfailing treasure for mortals;
those who get it obtain friendship with God,
commended for the gifts that come
    from instruction.

A time of silence may be observed.

Proverbs 31:26, 29, 31

She opens her mouth with wisdom,
and the teaching of kindness is on her tongue.
Many women have done excellently,
but you surpass them all.
Give her a share in the fruit of her hands,
and let her works praise her in the city gates.

A time of silence may be observed.

Antiphon for the Song of Hannah

Those who eat of wisdom will hunger for God,
and those who drink of wisdom will thirst
for more.

Continue with the Song of Hannah.

SONG OF HANNAH   *1 Samuel 2:1b–2, 5, 7–9*

My heart exults in the LORD,
my strength is exalted in my God.
My mouth derides my enemies,
because I rejoice in my victory.

There is no Holy One like the LORD,
no one besides you;
there is no Rock like our God.

Those who were full have hired themselves out
for bread,
but those who were hungry are fat with spoil.
The barren has borne seven,
but she who has many children is forlorn.

The LORD makes poor and makes rich;
God brings low but also exalts.
The Most High raises up the poor from the dust,
lifts the needy from the ash heap,
to make them sit with princes
and inherit a seat of honor.

For the pillars of the earth are the LORD's,
and on them God has set the world.
The Most High will guard the feet
of the faithful ones,
but the wicked shall be cut off in darkness;
for not by might does one prevail.

The antiphon is repeated.

LITANY OF PRAISE

Response to each invocation:
May we be your dwelling place.

Christ, Wisdom:
Christ, faithful word:
Christ, word of blessing:
Christ, word of challenge:
Christ, compassionate healer:
Christ, prophetic speaker:
Christ, clever teacher:
Christ, challenge to the powerful:
Christ, encouragement to the simple:
Christ, joy of all who seek wisdom:
Christ, gracious host, gracious guest:
Christ, our banquet:
Christ, revelation of the holy:

LORD'S PRAYER

CLOSING PRAYER

Holy Lord, Wisdom and the giver
 of all wisdom,
set for us this day the banquet of your word;
invite us to feast on the genius and beauty
that are all around us.
Turn us then in humility toward the poor
and toward those who suffer oppression
and toward the weak.
We ask this in Jesus' name,
who is Lord for ever and ever.
~Amen.

BLESSING

Let us bless the Lord.
~Thanks be to God.

SIGN OF PEACE

EVENING PRAYER

If a preparation rite is used, this verse is spoken or chanted:
> Rejoice!
> Jesus Christ is the light of the world:
> A light no darkness can extinguish.

OPENING VERSE

> Whoever loves Wisdom loves life;
> those who seek Wisdom are filled with joy.
> Those who serve Wisdom minister
>   to the Holy One.

SONG

> A starry flame throughout the night
> to guide all paths to God's delight:
> May Wisdom be our shining guide
> and travel always by our side.

> As countless as the drops of rain,
> her depth and height and breadth remain.
> From blossom time to ripened fruits,
> she nourishes all just pursuits.

> The discipline her rule ordains
> unfetters us from folly's chains.
> Her yoke that puts us to the test
> restores our souls and grants us rest.

Hid from the proud, shown to the meek,
her truth will bless all those who seek:
both male and female, bond and free,
made one in Christ eternally.

LM (88.88)

EVENING THANKSGIVING

Blessed are you, O God, abiding Wisdom.
~*Blessed are you, O God.*

In the beginning you created holy Wisdom,
who teaches her children,
gives help to those who seek her,
and blesses those who hold her fast.
~*Blessed are you, O God.*

In the course of time you gave us Jesus,
in whom Wisdom renews the face of the earth
in forgiveness and in delight.
~*Blessed are you, O God.*

Today we are called by your Spirit,
whose groans echo the cries of the poor,
to speak truth even to the powerful
and gentle words to the weary.
~*Blessed are you, O God.*

FIRST PSALM/CANTICLE

Sirach 24:13–22

Wisdom praises herself.

I grew tall like a cedar in Lebanon,
and like a cypress on the heights of Hermon.
I grew tall like a palm tree in En-gedi,
and like rosebushes in Jericho;
like a fair olive tree in the field,
and like a plane tree beside water I grew tall.

Like cassia and camel's thorn I gave
    forth perfume,
and like choice myrrh I spread my fragrance,
like galbanum, onycha, and stacte,
and like the odor of incense in the tent.

Like a terebinth I spread out my branches,
and my branches are glorious and graceful.
Like a vine I bud forth delights,
and my blossoms become glorious and
    abundant fruit.

Come to me, you who desire me,
and eat your fill of my fruits.
For the memory of me is sweeter than honey,
and the possession of me sweeter than
    the honeycomb.

Those who eat of me will hunger for more,
and those who drink of me will thirst for more.
Whoever obeys me will not be put to shame,
and those who work with me will not sin.

A time of silence may be observed.

SECOND PSALM/CANTICLE, READING AND ANTIPHON

The second psalm/canticle, the reading and the antiphon for the Song of Mary are arranged according to the days of the week.

SUNDAY

Sirach 1:1–10

Wisdom was created before all other things.

All wisdom is from the Lord,
and with God it remains forever.

The sand of the sea, the drops of rain,
and the days of eternity—who can count them?

The height of heaven, the breadth of the earth,
the abyss and wisdom—who can search
them out?

Wisdom was created before all other things,
and prudent understanding from eternity.

The root of wisdom—to whom has it
    been revealed?
Her subtleties—who knows them?

There is but one who is wise, greatly
    to be feared,
seated upon the throne—the Lord.

It is God who created her;
God saw her and took her measure;
God poured her out upon all created works,
upon all the living according to God's gift;
God lavished her upon those who love God.

A time of silence may be observed.

Luke 1:41–42, 45

When Elizabeth heard Mary's greeting, the child
leaped in her womb. And Elizabeth was filled
with the Holy Spirit and exclaimed with a loud
cry, "Blessed are you among women, and
blessed is the fruit of your womb. And blessed
is she who believed that there would be a ful-
fillment of what was spoken to her by the Lord."

A time of silence may be observed.

Antiphon for the Song of Mary

Blessed are the poor in spirit,
for theirs is the realm of heaven.

Continue with the Song of Mary, page 136.

MONDAY

Sirach 1:14–20

Wisdom is created with the faithful in the womb.

To fear the Lord is the beginning of wisdom;
she is created with the faithful in the womb.

She made among human beings
     an eternal foundation,
and among their descendants she will
     abide faithfully.

To fear the Lord is fullness of wisdom;
she inebriates mortals with her fruits;
she fills their whole house with desirable goods,
and their storehouses with her produce.

The fear of the Lord is the crown of wisdom,
making peace and perfect health to flourish.

She rained down knowledge and
  discerning comprehension,
and she heightened the glory of those who held
  her fast.

To fear the Lord is the root of wisdom,
and her branches are long life.

A time of silence may be observed.

Luke 1:26a, 27ac–28, 34–35a, 38a

In the sixth month the angel Gabriel was sent
by God to a virgin whose name was Mary. And
he came to her and said, "Greetings, favored
one! The Lord is with you." Mary said to the
angel, "How can this be, since I am a virgin?"
The angel said to her, "The Holy Spirit will
come upon you." Then Mary said, "Here am
I, the servant of the Lord; let it be with me
according to your word."

A time of silence may be observed.

Antiphon for the Song of Mary

Blessed are those who mourn,
for they will be comforted.

Continue with the Song of Mary, page 136.

TUESDAY

Sirach 4:11–18

Wisdom teaches her children.

Wisdom teaches her children
and gives help to those who seek her.

Whoever loves her loves life,
and those who seek her from early morning
    are filled with joy.

Whoever holds her fast inherits glory,
and the Lord blesses the place she enters.

Those who serve her minister to the Holy One;
the Lord loves those who love her.

Those who obey her will judge the nations,
and all who listen to her will live secure.

If they remain faithful, they will inherit her;
their descendants will also obtain her.

For at first she will walk with them
    on tortuous paths;
she will bring fear and dread upon them,
and will torment them by her discipline
until she trusts them,
and she will test them with her ordinances.

Then she will come straight back to them again
   and gladden them,
and will reveal her secrets to them.

A time of silence may be observed.

Matthew 11:18–19, 25

Jesus said, "John came neither eating nor
drinking, and they say, 'He has a demon'; the
Son of Man came eating and drinking, and
they say, 'Look a glutton and a drunkard, a
friend of tax collectors and sinners!' Yet wisdom
is vindicated by her deeds." At that time Jesus
said, "I thank you, Father, Lord of heaven and
earth, because you have hidden these things
from the wise and the intelligent and have
revealed them to infants."

A time of silence may be observed.

Antiphon for the Song of Mary

Blessed are the meek,
for they will inherit the earth.

Continue with the Song of Mary, page 136.

WEDNESDAY

Sirach 6:22–31

Wisdom's yoke is a golden ornament.

For wisdom is like her name;
she is not readily perceived by many.

Listen, my child, and accept my judgment;
do not reject my counsel.

Put your feet into her fetters,
and your neck into her collar.

Bend your shoulders and carry her,
and do not fret under her bonds.

Come to her with all your soul,
and keep her ways with all your might.

Search out and seek, and she will become
    known to you;
and when you get hold of her, do not let her go.

For at last you will find the rest she gives,
and she will be changed into joy for you.

Then her fetters will become for you
    a strong defense,
and her collar a glorious robe.

Her yoke is a golden ornament,
and her bonds a purple cord.

You will wear her like a glorious robe,
and put her on like a splendid crown.

A time of silence may be observed.

Matthew 5:1–3

When Jesus saw the crowds, he went up the
mountain; and after he sat down, his disciples
came to him. Then he began to speak, and
taught them, saying: "Blessed are the poor in
spirit, for theirs is the kingdom of heaven."

A time of silence may be observed.

Antiphon for the Song of Mary

Blessed are those who hunger and thirst
    for righteousness,
for they will be filled.

Continue with the Song of Mary, page 136.

Thursday

Sirach 51:12b–20a

I sought wisdom in my prayer.

I thank you and praise you,
and I bless the name of the Lord.

While I was still young, before I went
on my travels,
I sought wisdom openly in my prayer.

Before the temple I asked for her,
and I will search for her until the end.

From the first blossom to the ripening grape
my heart delighted in her;
my foot walked on the straight path;
from my youth I followed her steps.

I inclined my ear a little and received her,
and I found for myself much instruction.

I made progress in her;
to the one who gives wisdom I will give glory.

For I resolved to live according to wisdom,
and I was zealous for the good,
and I shall never be disappointed.

My soul grappled with wisdom
and in my conduct I was strict.

I spread out my hands to the heavens,
and lamented my ignorance of her.

I directed my soul to her,
and in purity I found her.

A time of silence may be observed.

Luke 10:38–39

Now as they went on their way, Jesus entered
a certain village, where a woman named Martha
welcomed him into her home. She had a sister
named Mary, who sat the Lord's feet and
listened to what he was saying.

A time of silence may be observed.

Antiphon for the Song of Mary

Blessed are the merciful,
for they will receive mercy.

Continue with the Song of Mary, page 136.

FRIDAY

Wisdom of Solomon 9:9–11, 13, 17–18

Wisdom was present when God made the earth.

With you is wisdom, she who knows
    your works
and was present when you made the world;
she understands what is pleasing in your sight
and what is right according to
    your commandments.

Send her forth from the holy heavens,
and from the throne of your glory send her,
that she may labor at my side,
and that I may learn what is pleasing to you.

For she knows and understands all things,
and she will guide me wisely in my actions
and guard me with her glory.

For who can learn the counsel of God?
Or who can discern what the Lord wills?

Who has learned your counsel,
unless you have given wisdom
and sent your holy spirit from on high?

And thus the paths of those on earth were
    set right,
and people were taught what pleases you,
and were saved by wisdom.

A time of silence may be observed.

James 3:17–18

But the wisdom from above is first pure, then
peaceable, gentle, willing to yield, full of mercy
and good fruits, without a trace of partiality
or hypocrisy. And a harvest of righteousness
is sown in peace for those who make peace.

A time of silence may be observed.

Antiphon for the Song of Mary

Blessed are the pure in heart,
for they will see God.

Continue with the Song of Mary, page 136

SATURDAY

Wisdom of Solomon 10:15–21

Wisdom became a starry flame through the night.

A holy people and blameless race
wisdom delivered from a nation of oppressors.

She entered the soul of a servant of the Lord,
and withstood dread kings with wonders
   and signs.

She gave to holy people the reward
   of their labors;
she guided them along a marvelous way,
and became a shelter to them by day,
and a starry flame through the night.

She brought them over the Red Sea,
and led them through deep waters;
but she drowned their enemies,
and cast them up from the depth of the sea.

Therefore the righteous plundered the ungodly;
they sang hymns, O Lord, to your holy name,
and praised with one accord your
   defending hand;
for wisdom opened the mouths of those
   who were mute,
and made the tongues of infants speak clearly.

A time of silence may be observed.

Galatians 3:26–28

In Christ Jesus you are all children of God
through faith. As many of you as were baptized
into Christ have clothed yourselves with Christ.
There is no longer Jew or Greek, there is no
longer slave or free, there is no longer male and
female; for all of you are one in Christ Jesus.

A time of silence may be observed.

Antiphon for the Song of Mary

Blessed are the peacemakers,
for they will be called children of God.

Continue with the Song of Mary.

SONG OF MARY   *Luke 2:47–55*

My soul proclaims the greatness of the Lord,
my spirit rejoices in God my Savior,
for you, Lord, have looked with favor
    on your lowly servant.

From this day all generations will call
    me blessed:
you, the Almighty, have done great things for me
and holy is your name.
You have mercy on those who fear you,
from generation to generation.

You have shown strength with your arm
and scattered the proud in their conceit,
casting down the mighty from their thrones
and lifting up the lowly.
You have filled the hungry with good things
and sent the rich away empty.

You have come to the aid of your servant Israel,
to remember the promise of mercy,
the promise made to our forebears,
to Abraham and his children for ever.

The antiphon is repeated.

INTERCESSIONS

℣Response to each invocation:
    Lord, have mercy.

That your wisdom give us life:
That your wisdom dwell in our hearts:
That your wisdom feed us and give us drink:
That your wisdom be for us like honey:
That your wisdom guide those in power:

That peace may flourish:
That parents and teachers find joy in children:
That the weary find rest:
That those in danger find safety:
That prisoners be set free:
That refugees find a home:
That our lips may ever sing God's praise:
That the sick be comforted:
That the dying find peace:

LORD'S PRAYER

CLOSING PRAYER

How shall we ever find wisdom, loving God,
unless we seek you in the lowly, whom you love,
and attend to you in children and in the weak?
Give us this evening eyes to see
and ears to hear what is about us always:
the holy wisdom that dwells
with your friends and your prophets.
We ask this in Jesus' name,
who is Lord for ever and ever.
~*Amen.*

BLESSING

May the compassionate and merciful God
give us a restful night
and peace at the last.
~*Amen.*

SIGN OF PEACE

THE CREATOR
AND CREATION

At Morning Prayer, the psalms praise the creator and speak of creation. The scripture passages all speak of creation. The antiphons for the Song of Hannah are taken from the Benedicite, the hymn of creation found in the book of Daniel.

At Evening Prayer, the psalms also describe creation and praise the creator. The scripture readings tell of the seven days of creation, and the antiphons for the Song of Mary are again taken from the Benedicite.

MORNING PRAYER

If a preparation rite is used, this verse is spoken or chanted:
> Give thanks!
> God saw everything that had been made,
> and indeed, it was very good.

OPENING VERSE

> The heavens proclaim the glory of God!
> And the cosmos shows forth the work
>   of God's hand.
> Day unto day takes up the story,
> and night unto night makes known the message.

SONG

> From tents of night the sun comes forth
> to run its joyful course,
> as rocks cleave into flowing brooks
> sprung from a boundless source.
>
> The God who waters all the earth
> for fruits and flowering trees
> sets limits to the broad abyss
> and gathers up the seas.

God thunders with a mighty voice
and flashes flames of fire.
The earth falls trembling to its knees
in awed and hushed desire.

In storm-dark clouds, the mountains melt;
the wind-whipped forest whirls,
'til God's own hand strews seeds of light
like incandescent pearls.

Endowing creatures great and small
with life and livelihood,
God forms them with a word of pow'r
and calls creation "Good!"

With jubilance of heav'nly choirs,
with lyre and harp and string,
we rise at dawn to join the song
glad Judah's daughters sing.

CM (86.86.)

MORNING THANKSGIVING

O God, you are the source of all creation.
~*Accept our morning thanks and praise.*

We give you thanks for darkness and light,
which mark the rhythms of our lives,
for the sky that envelops and embraces us,
for the clouds that dance across the heavens,
for the oceans and the land,
for crafting us with ingenuity, beauty and humor.
~*Accept our morning thanks and praise.*

We give you thanks for Jesus,
sun of justice, bread of life, living water,
wisdom who played before you
    in the beginning.
~*Accept our morning thanks and praise.*

We give you thanks for the Holy Spirit,
promised gift who inspires us
with care for all creation.
~*Accept our morning thanks and praise.*

FIRST PSALM/CANTICLE

Proverbs 8:22–31

God created wisdom at the beginning.

The LORD created me at the beginning
    of the divine work,
the first of God's acts of long ago.

Ages ago I was set up,
at the first, before the beginning of the earth.

When there were no depths I was brought forth,
when there were no springs abounding
     with water.

Before the mountains had been shaped,
before the hills, I was brought forth—
when God had not yet made earth and fields,
or the world's first bits of soil.

When the heavens were established, I was there,
when God drew a circle on the face of the deep,
when the skies above were made firm,
when the foundations of the deep
     were established,

when God assigned to the sea its limit,
so that the waters might not transgress
     God's command,
when the foundations of the earth were
     marked out,
then I was beside God, like a master worker;

and I was daily God's delight,
rejoicing before God always,
rejoicing in the inhabited world
and delighting in the human race.

A time of silence may be observed.

SECOND PSALM/CANTICLE, READING AND ANTIPHON

The second psalm/canticle, the reading and the antiphon for the Song of Hannah are arranged according to the days of the week.

SUNDAY

Psalm 8

How majestic is God's name in all the earth.

How great is your name, O LORD our God,
through all the earth!

Your majesty is praised above the heavens;
on the lips of children and of babes
you have found praise to foil your enemy,
to silence the foe and the rebel.

When I see the heavens, the work of your hands,
the moon and the stars which you arranged,
what are we that you should keep us in mind,
mere mortals that you care for us?

Yet you have made us little less than gods;
and crowned us with glory and honor,
you gave us power over the work of your hands,
put all things under our feet.

All of them, sheep and cattle,
yes, even the savage beasts,
birds of the air, and fish
that make their way through the waters.

How great is your name, O LORD our God,
through all the earth!

A time of silence may be observed.

John 1:1–4

In the beginning was the Word, and the Word
was with God, and the Word was God. The
Word was in the beginning with God. All things
came into being through the Word, and without
the Word not one thing came into being. What
has come into being in the Word was life, and
the life was the light of all people.

A time of silence may be observed.

Antiphon for the Song of Hannah

Bless God, sun and moon.
Bless God, stars of heaven.
Sing praise to the Holy One.

Continue with the Song of Hannah, page 159.

MONDAY

Psalm 19:2–7

The heavens proclaim the glory of God.

The heavens proclaim the glory of God,
and the firmament shows forth the work
   of God's hands.
Day unto day takes up the story
and night unto night makes known the message.

No speech, no word, no voice is heard
yet their span extends through all the earth,
their words to the utmost bounds of the world.

There God has placed a tent for the sun;
it comes forth like a bridegroom coming
   from his tent,
rejoices like a champion to run its course.

At the end of the sky is the rising of the sun;
to the furthest end of the sky is its course.
There is nothing concealed from its
   burning heat.

A time of silence may be observed.

Romans 8:19–23

For the creation waits with eager longing for
the revealing of the children of God; for the

creation was subjected to futility, not of its own will but by the will of the one who subjected it, in hope that the creation itself will be set free from its bondage to decay and will obtain the freedom of the glory of the children of God. We know that the whole creation has been groaning in labor pains until now, and not only the creation but we ourselves, who have the first fruits of the Spirit, groan inwardly while we wait for adoption, the redemption of our bodies.

A time of silence may be observed.

Antiphon for the Song of Hannah

Bless God, all rain and dew.
Bless God, all you winds.
Sing praise to the Holy One.

Continue with the Song of Hannah, page 159.

Tuesday

Psalm 29

God sits enthroned over the flood.

O give the LORD, you children of God,
give the LORD glory and power;
give the LORD the glory of the Name.
Adore the LORD, resplendent and holy.

The LORD's voice resounding on the waters,
the LORD on the immensity of waters,
the voice of the LORD, full of power,
the voice of the LORD, full of splendor.

The LORD's voice shattering the cedars,
the LORD shatters the cedars of Lebanon,
makes Lebanon leap like a calf
and Sirion like a young wild ox.

The LORD's voice flashes flames of fire.

The LORD's voice shaking the wilderness,
the LORD shakes the wilderness of Kadesh;
the LORD's voice rending the oak tree
and stripping the forest bare.

The God of glory thunders.
In this temple they all cry: "Glory!"
The LORD sat enthroned over the flood;
the LORD sits as king for ever.

The LORD will give strength to the people,
the LORD will bless the people with peace.

A time of silence may be observed.

2 Corinthians 5:17–18

So if anyone is in Christ, there is a new creation:
everything old has passed away; see, everything
has become new! All this is from God, who

reconciled us through Christ, and has given us the ministry of reconciliation.

A time of silence may be observed.

Antiphon for the Song of Hannah

Bless God, all you winds.
Bless God, fire and heat.
Sing praise to the Holy One.

Continue with the Song of Hannah, page 159.

WEDNESDAY

Psalm 33:1–9, 20–22

By God's word the heavens were made.

Ring out your joy to the LORD, O you just;
for praise is fitting for loyal hearts.

Give thanks to the LORD upon the harp,
with a ten-stringed lute play your songs.
Sing to the Lord a song that is new,
play loudly, with all your skill.

For the word of the LORD is faithful,
and all God's works are done in truth.
The LORD loves justice and right
and fills the earth with love.

By God's word the heavens were made
by the breath of God's mouth all the stars.
God collects the waves of the ocean;
and stores up the depths of the sea.

Let all the earth fear the LORD,
all who live in the world stand in awe.
For God spoke; it came to be.
God commanded; it sprang into being.

Our soul is waiting for the LORD.
The LORD is our help and our shield.
Our hearts find joy in the LORD.
We trust in God's holy name.

May your love be upon us, O LORD,
as we place all our hope in you.

A time of silence may be observed.

Colossians 1:15–16

Christ is the image of the invisible God, the
firstborn of all creation; for in him all things in
heaven and on earth were created, things visible
and invisible, whether thrones or dominions or
rulers or powers—all things have been created
through him and for him.

A time of silence may be observed.

Antiphon for the Song of Hannah

Bless God, winter cold and summer heat.
Bless God, dews and falling snow.
Sing praise to the Holy One.

Continue with the Song of Hannah, page 159.

THURSDAY

Psalm 74:12–23

The day and night are God's.

God is our king from time past,
the giver of help through all the land.
It was you who divided the sea by your might,
who shattered the heads of the monsters
   in the sea.

It was you who crushed Leviathan's heads
and gave him as food to the untamed beasts.
It was you who opened springs and torrents;
it was you who dried up ever-flowing rivers.

Yours is the day and yours is the night.
It was you who appointed the light and the sun;
it was you who fixed the bounds of the earth,
you who made both summer and winter.

Remember this, LORD, and see
　　the enemy scoffing;
a senseless people insults your name.
Do not give Israel, your dove, to the hawk
nor forget the life of your poor ones for ever.

Remember your covenant; every cave in the land
is a place where violence makes its home.
Do not let the oppressed return disappointed;
let the poor and the needy bless your name.

Arise, O God, and defend your cause!
Remember how the senseless revile you
　　all the day.
Do not forget the clamor of your foes,
the daily increasing uproar of your foes.

A time of silence may be observed.

Colossians 3:10–11

You have clothed yourselves with the new self,
which is being renewed in knowledge according
to the image of its creator. In that renewal there
is no longer Greek and Jew, circumcised and
uncircumcised, barbarian, Scythian, slave and
free; but Christ is all and in all!

A time of silence may be observed.

Antiphon for the Song of Hannah

Bless God, nights and days.
Bless God, light and darkness.
Sing praise to the Holy One.

Continue with the Song of Hannah, page 159.

FRIDAY

Psalm 95:1–7a

The sea is God's, and the dry land.

Come, ring out our joy to the LORD;
hail the rock who saves us.
Let us come before God, giving thanks,
with songs let us hail the Lord.

A mighty God is the LORD,
a great king above all gods,
in whose hands are the depths of the earth,
the heights of the mountains as well.
The sea belongs to God, who made it,
and the dry land shaped by God's hands.

Come in; let us bow and bend low;
let us kneel before the God who made us,
for this is our God and we
the people who belong to God's pasture,
the flock that is led by the LORD's hand.

A time of silence may be observed.

Ephesians 2:8–10

For by grace you have been saved through faith,
and this is not your own doing; it is the gift of
God—not the result of works, so that no one
may boast. For we are what God has made us,
created in Christ Jesus for good works, which
God prepared beforehand to be our way of life.

A time of silence may be observed.

Antiphon for the Song of Hannah

Bless God, ice and cold.
Bless God, frosts and snows.
Sing praise to the Holy One.

Continue with the Song of Hannah, page 159.

SATURDAY

Psalm 97

The skies proclaim God's justice.

The LORD is king, let earth rejoice,
let all the coastlands be glad.
Surrounded by cloud and darkness,
justice and right, God's throne.

A fire prepares the way;
it burns up foes on every side.
God's lightnings light up the world,
the earth trembles at the sight.

The mountains melt like wax
before the LORD of all the earth.
The skies proclaim God's justice;
all peoples see God's glory.

Let those who serve idols be ashamed,
those who boast of their worthless gods.
All you spirits, worship the Lord.

Zion hears and is glad;
the people of Judah rejoice
because of your judgements, O LORD.

For you indeed are the LORD
most high above all the earth,
exalted far above all spirits.

The LORD loves those who hate evil,
guards the souls of the saints,
and sets them free from the wicked.

Light shines forth for the just
and joy for the upright of heart.
Rejoice, you just, in the LORD;
give glory to God's holy name.

A time of silence may be observed.

Revelation 4:11

You are worthy, our Lord and God,
to receive glory and honor and power,
for you created all things,
and by your will they existed and were created.

A time of silence may be observed.

Antiphon for the Song of Hannah

Bless God, lightning and clouds.
Bless God, mountains and hills.
Sing praise to the Holy One.

Continue with the Song of Hannah.

SONG OF HANNAH *1 Samuel 2:1b–2, 5, 7–9*

My heart exults in the LORD,
my strength is exalted in my God.
My mouth derides my enemies,
because I rejoice in my victory.

There is no Holy One like the LORD,
no one besides you;
there is no Rock like our God.

Those who were full have hired themselves out
    for bread,
but those who were hungry are fat with spoil.
The barren has borne seven,
but she who has many children is forlorn.

The LORD makes poor and makes rich;
God brings low but also exalts.
The Most High raises up the poor from the dust,
lifts the needy from the ash heap,
to make them sit with princes
and inherit a seat of honor.

For the pillars of the earth are the LORD's,
and on them God has set the world.
The Most High will guard the feet
    of the faithful ones,
but the wicked shall be cut off in darkness;
for not by might does one prevail.

The antiphon is repeated.

LITANY OF PRAISE

Response to each invocation:
   ~*We tell of your glory.*

   Christ, firstborn of creation:
   Christ, image of God:
   Christ, gift of God:
   Christ, love song of God:
   Christ, morning star:
   Christ, creating word:
   Christ, liberating from bondage:
   Christ, lighting our way:
   Christ, caring for all in need:
   Christ, reconciling all with God:
   Christ, giving all your peace:
   Christ, sending the creating Spirit:
   Christ, loving justice:
   Christ, the way, the truth and the life:
   Christ, all in all:

LORD'S PRAYER

CLOSING PRAYER

From the beauty of darkness
to the beauty of light
we come again, creating God,
and from the praise of sleep
to the praise of waking.
Give us this day some portion in your work,
for we are your image
and so we must create
what will be good in your sight.
We ask this in Jesus' name,
who is Lord for ever and ever.
~Amen.

BLESSING

Let us bless the Lord.
~Thanks be to God.

SIGN OF PEACE

If a preparation rite is used, this verse is spoken or chanted:
Jesus Christ is the light of the world:
A light no darkness can extinguish.

OPENING VERSE

Let us come before God, giving thanks.
With songs let us praise the Most High.
By God's word the heavens were made,
by the breath of God's mouth all the stars.

SONG

As azure shades to cobalt blue
and dusk enfolds the skies,
we turn our prayerful hearts to you,
creating God, most wise.

By Wisdom you brought forth the earth,
from depths to vaults of heav'n.
By sovereign word, you grant new birth
where spacious life is giv'n.

The moon that rules the teeming night
gleams bright with silver flame.
The stars that spangle heaven's height
you number and you name.

As ev'ning falls by your design,
its banners soon unfurled,
so let our lamps in darkness shine
as light for all the world.

CM (86.86)

EVENING THANKSGIVING

Blessed are you, O God, weaver of the universe.
~Blessed are you, O God.

The first verse of the blessing changes with the day of the week.
The second and third verses are the same each day.

SUNDAY

In the beginning, on the first day,
you created the heavens and the earth.
You said, "Let there be light,"
and you saw that it was good.
~Blessed are you, O God.

In the course of time you gave us Jesus,
whose prophet proclaimed a new creation:
"I saw the holy city, the new Jerusalem,
coming down from God,
prepared as a bride adorned for her husband."
~Blessed are you, O God.

Today we are created anew by your Spirit
to see and to hear,
to taste and to smell and to touch your goodness,
and to do as you have done.
~*Blessed are you, O God.*

Monday

In the beginning, on the second day,
you created a dome to separate the waters
    from the waters.
You called the dome Sky,
and you saw that it was good.
~*Blessed are you, O God.*

In the course of time you gave us Jesus,
whose prophet proclaimed a new creation:
"I saw the holy city, the new Jerusalem,
coming down from God,
prepared as a bride adorned for her husband."
~*Blessed are you, O God.*

Today we are created anew by your Spirit
to see and to hear,
to taste and to smell and to touch your goodness,
and to do as you have done.
~*Blessed are you, O God.*

TUESDAY

In the beginning, on the third day,
you gathered the waters together and let dry
   land appear.
By your word the earth brought forth plants
   and trees of every kind,
and you saw that it was good.
~*Blessed are you, O God.*

In the course of time you gave us Jesus,
whose prophet proclaimed a new creation:
"I saw the holy city, the new Jerusalem,
coming down from God,
prepared as a bride adorned for her husband."
~*Blessed are you, O God.*

Today we are created anew by your Spirit
to see and to hear,
to taste and to smell and to touch your goodness,
and to do as you have done.
~*Blessed are you, O God.*

WEDNESDAY

In the beginning, on the fourth day,
you created the sun, the moon and the stars,
to separate the day from the night
and to mark the days, years and seasons,
and you saw that it was good.
~*Blessed are you, O God.*

In the course of time you gave us Jesus,
whose prophet proclaimed a new creation:
"I saw the holy city, the new Jerusalem,
coming down from God,
prepared as a bride adorned for her husband."
~*Blessed are you, O God.*

Today we are created anew by your Spirit
to see and to hear,
to taste and to smell and to touch your goodness,
and to do as you have done.
~*Blessed are you, O God.*

THURSDAY

In the beginning, on the fifth day,
you created all the living creatures
    of sea and sky;
you blessed them,
and you saw that it was good.
~*Blessed are you, O God.*

In the course of time you gave us Jesus,
whose prophet proclaimed a new creation:
"I saw the holy city, the new Jerusalem,
coming down from God,
prepared as a bride adorned for her husband."
~*Blessed are you, O God.*

Today we are created anew by your Spirit
to see and to hear,
to taste and to smell and to touch your goodness,
and to do as you have done.
~Blessed are you, O God.

FRIDAY

In the beginning, on the sixth day,
you created the animals of the earth,
and you made humankind in your image,
and you saw that it was good.
~Blessed are you, O God.

In the course of time you gave us Jesus,
whose prophet proclaimed a new creation:
"I saw the holy city, the new Jerusalem,
coming down from God,
prepared as a bride adorned for her husband."
~Blessed are you, O God.

Today we are created anew by your Spirit
to see and to hear,
to taste and to smell and to touch your goodness,
and to do as you have done.
~Blessed are you, O God.

In the beginning, on the seventh day,
you rested from all the work that you had done.
You blessed the seventh day and made it holy,
and you saw that all was good.
~*Blessed are you, O God.*

In the course of time you gave us Jesus,
whose prophet proclaimed a new creation:
"I saw the holy city, the new Jerusalem,
coming down from God,
prepared as a bride adorned for her husband."
~*Blessed are you, O God.*

Today we are created anew by your Spirit
to see and to hear,
to taste and to smell and to touch your goodness,
and to do as you have done.
~*Blessed are you, O God.*

FIRST PSALM/CANTICLE

Isaiah 49:13–18

God will remember like a mother.

Sing for joy, O heavens, and exult, O earth;
break forth, O mountains, into singing!
For the LORD has comforted the people,
and will have compassion on God's
    suffering ones.

But Zion said, "The LORD has forsaken me,
my Lord has forgotten me."

Can a woman forget her nursing child,
or show no compassion for the child
    of her womb?
Even these may forget,
yet I will not forget you.

See, I have inscribed you on the palms
    of my hands;
your walls are continually before me.
Your builders outdo your destroyers,
and those who laid you waste go away from you.

Lift up your eyes all around and see;
they all gather, they come to you.
As I live, says the LORD,
you shall put all of them on like an ornament,
and like a bride you shall bind them on.

A time of silence may be observed.

SECOND PSALM/CANTICLE, READING AND ANTIPHON

The second psalm/canticle, the reading and the antiphon for the Song of Mary are arranged according to the days of the week.

SUNDAY

Psalm 103:1–2, 15–22

God rules over all.

My soul, give thanks to the LORD,
all my being, bless God's holy name.
My soul, give thanks to the LORD
and never forget all God's blessings.

As for us, our days are like grass;
we flower like the flower of the field;
the wind blows and we are gone
and our place never sees us again.

But the love of the LORD is everlasting
upon those who fear the Lord.
God's justice reaches out to children's children
when they keep the covenant in truth,
when they keep God's will in their mind.

The LORD's throne is set in heaven
and God's realm rules over all.
Give thanks to the LORD, all you angels,
mighty in power, fulfilling God's word,
who heed the voice of that word.

Give thanks to the LORD, all you hosts,
you servants who do God's will.
Give thanks to the LORD, all that exists,
in every place where God rules.
My soul, give thanks to the LORD!

A time of silence may be observed.

Genesis 1:1–5

In the beginning when God created the heavens
and the earth, the earth was a formless void
and darkness covered the face of the deep, while
a wind from God swept over the face of the
waters. Then God said, "Let there be light";
and there was light. And God saw that the light
was good; and God separated the light from
the darkness. God called the light Day, and the
darkness God called Night. And there was
evening and there was morning, the first day.

A time of silence may be observed.

Antiphon for the Song of Mary

Bless God, all that grows in the ground.
Bless God, seas and rivers.
Sing praise to the Holy One.

Continue with the Song of Mary, page 184.

MONDAY

Psalm 104:1–12

God makes a chariot of the clouds.

Bless the LORD, my soul!
LORD God, how great you are,
clothed in majesty and glory,
wrapped in light as in a robe!

You stretch out the heavens like a tent.
Above the rains you build your dwelling.
You make the clouds your chariot,
you walk on the wings of the wind;
you make the winds your messengers
and flashing fire your servants.

You founded the earth on its base,
to stand firm from age to age.
You wrapped it with the ocean like a cloak:
the waters stood higher than the mountains.

At your threat they took to flight;
at the voice of your thunder they fled.
They rose over the mountains and flowed down
to the place which you had appointed.
You set limits they might not pass
lest they return to cover the earth.

You make springs gush forth in the valleys;
they flow in between the hills.
They give drink to all the beasts of the field;
the wild asses quench their thirst.
On their banks dwell the birds of heaven;
from the branches they sing their song.

A time of silence may be observed.

Genesis 1:6–8

And God said, "Let there be a dome in the
midst of the waters, and let it separate the
waters from the waters." So God made the
dome and separated the waters that were under
the dome from the waters that were above the
dome. And it was so. God called the dome Sky.
And there was evening and there was morning,
the second day.

A time of silence may be observed.

Antiphon for the Song of Mary

Bless God, you springs.
Bless God, you whales and all that swim
   in the waters.
Sing praise to the Holy One.

Continue with the Song of Mary, page 184.

TUESDAY

Psalm 104:24–35

The earth is full of God's creations.

How many are your works, O LORD!
In wisdom you have made them all.
The earth is full of your riches.

There is the sea, vast and wide,
with its moving swarms past counting,
living things great and small.
The ships are moving there
and the monsters you made to play with.

All of these look to you
to give them their food in due season.
You give it, they gather it up;
you open your hand, they have their fill.

You hide your face, they are dismayed;
you take back your spirit, they die,
returning to the dust from which they came.
You send forth your spirit, they are created;
and you renew the face of the earth.

May the glory of the LORD last for ever!
May the LORD rejoice in creation!
God looks on the earth and it trembles;
at God's touch, the mountains send forth smoke.

I will sing to the LORD all my life,
make music to my God while I live.
May my thoughts be pleasing to God.
I find my joy in the LORD.
Let sinners vanish from the earth
and the wicked exist no more.

Bless the LORD, my soul.

A time of silence may be observed.

Genesis 1:9–11, 13

And God said, "Let the waters under the sky be gathered together into one place, and let the dry land appear." And it was so. God called the dry land Earth, and the waters that were gathered together God called Seas. And God saw that it was good. Then God said, "Let the earth put forth vegetation: plants yielding seed, and fruit trees of every kind on earth that bear fruit with the seed in it." And it was so. And there was evening and there was morning, the third day.

A time of silence may be observed.

Antiphon for the Song of Mary

Bless God, all birds of the air.
Bless God, all wild animals and cattle.
Sing praise to the Holy One.

Continue with the Song of Mary, page 184.

WEDNESDAY

Psalm 136:1–9

God made the great lights.

Alleluia!
O give thanks to the LORD who is good,
whose love endures forever.
Give thanks to the God of gods,
whose love endures forever.
Give thanks to the Lord of lords,
whose love endures forever;

who alone has wrought marvelous works,
whose love endures forever;
whose wisdom it was made the skies,
whose love endures forever;
who fixed the earth firmly on the seas,
whose love endures forever.

It was God who made the great lights,
whose love endures forever;
the sun to rule in the day,
whose love endures forever;
the moon and stars in the night,
whose love endures forever.

A time of silence may be observed.

Genesis 1:14–15, 19

And God said, "Let there be lights in the dome
of the sky to separate the day from the night;
and let them be for signs and for seasons and for
days and years, and let them be lights in the
dome of the sky to give light upon the earth."
And there was evening and there was morning,
the fourth day.

A time of silence may be observed.

Antiphon for the Song of Mary

Bless God, all people on earth.
Bless God, you friends of God.
Sing praise to the Holy One.

Continue with the Song of Mary, page 184.

Thursday

Psalm 146

God made heaven and earth.

Alleluia!

My soul, give praise to the LORD;
I will praise the LORD all my days,
make music to my God while I live.

Put no trust in the powerful,
mere morals in whom there is no help.
Take their breath, they return to clay,
and their plans that day come to nothing.

They are happy who are helped by Jacob's God,
whose hope is in the LORD their God,
who alone made heaven and earth,
the seas and all they contain.

It is the Lord who keeps faith for ever,
who is just to those who are oppressed.
It is God who gives bread to the hungry,
the LORD, who sets prisoners free,

the LORD who gives sight to the blind,
who raises up those who are bowed down,
the LORD, who protects the stranger
and upholds the widow and orphan.

It is the LORD who loves the just
but thwarts the path of the wicked.
The LORD will reign for ever,
Zion's God, from age to age.

Alleluia!

A time of silence may be observed.

Genesis 1:20–21a, 23

And God said, "Let the waters bring forth
swarms of living creatures, and let birds fly
above the earth across the dome of the sky." So
God created the great sea monsters and every
living creature that moves, of every kind, with
which the waters swarm, and every winged bird
of every kind. And there was evening and there
was morning, the fifth day.

A time of silence may be observed.

Antiphon for the Song of Mary

Bless God, spirits and souls of the righteous.
Bless God, you who are holy and humble
    in heart.
Sing praise to the Holy One.

Continue with the Song of Mary, page 184.

FRIDAY

Psalm 147:1, 4, 8–9, 15–20

God determines the number of the stars.

Alleluia!

Sing praise to the LORD who is good;
sing to our God who is loving:
to God our praise is due.

God fixes the number of the stars;
and calls each one by its name.

God covers the heavens with clouds,
and prepares the rain for the earth,
making mountains sprout with grass
and with plants to serve our needs.
God provides the beasts with their food
and the young ravens when they cry.

God sends out word to the earth
and swiftly runs the command.
God showers down snow white as wool,
and scatters hoarfrost like ashes.

God hurls down hailstones like crumbs,
and causes the waters to freeze.
God sends forth a word and it melts them:
at the breath of God's mouth the waters flow.

God makes his word known to Jacob,
to Israel laws and decrees.
God has not dealt thus with other nations,
has not taught them divine decrees.

Alleluia!

A time of silence may be observed.

Genesis 1:24, 27, 31

And God said, "Let the earth bring forth living
creatures of every kind: cattle and creeping
things and wild animals of the earth of every
kind." And it was so. And God created humankind in the divine image, in the image of God
God created them; male and female God created
them. God saw everything that had been made,
and indeed, it was very good. And there was
evening and there was morning, the sixth day.

A time of silence may be observed.

Antiphon for the Song of Mary

Bless God, you heavens.
Bless God, you angels.
Sing praise to the Holy One.

Continue with the Song of Mary, page 184.

Psalm 148

God commanded and all was created.

Alleluia!

Praise the LORD from the heavens,
praise God in the heights.
Praise God, all you angels,
praise God, all you host.

Praise God, sun and moon,
praise God, shining stars.
Praise God, highest heavens
and the waters above the heavens.

Let them praise the name of the LORD.
The Lord commanded: they were made.
God fixed them forever,
gave a law which shall not pass away.

Praise the LORD from the earth,
sea creatures and all oceans,
fire and hail, snow and mist,
stormy winds that obey God's word;

all mountain and hills,
all fruit trees and cedars,
beasts, wild and tame,
reptiles and birds on the wing;

all earth's nations and peoples,
earth's leaders and rulers;
young men and maidens,
the old together with children.

Let them praise the name of the LORD
who alone is exalted.
The splendor of God's name
reaches beyond heaven and earth.

God exalts the strength of the people,
is the praise of all the saints,
of the sons and daughters of Israel,
of the people to whom God comes close.

Alleluia!

A time of silence may be observed.

Genesis 2:1–3

Thus the heavens and the earth were finished,
and all their multitude. And on the seventh day
God finished the work that God had done, and
the Most High rested on the seventh day from
all the work that had been done. So God blessed
the seventh day and hallowed it, because on
it God rested from all the work that the Most
High had done in creation.

A time of silence may be observed.

Antiphon for the Song of Mary

Blessed are you, O God of our mothers and
    our fathers.
Blessed is your glorious, holy name.
Bless God, all you works of God.
Sing praise to the Holy One.

Continue with the Song of Mary.

SONG OF MARY   *Luke 2:47–55*

My soul proclaims the greatness of the Lord,
my spirit rejoices in God my Savior,
for you, Lord, have looked with favor
    on your lowly servant.

From this day all generations will call
    me blessed:
you, the Almighty, have done great things for me
and holy is your name.
You have mercy on those who fear you,
from generation to generation.

You have shown strength with your arm
and scattered the proud in their conceit,
casting down the mighty from their thrones
and lifting up the lowly.
You have filled the hungry with good things
and sent the rich away empty.

You have come to the aid of your servant Israel,
to remember the promise of mercy,
the promise made to our forebears,
to Abraham and his children for ever.

The antiphon is repeated.

INTERCESSIONS

Response to each invocation:
    Lord, have mercy.

That we live in creation with great thanks:
That we live in creation with great reverence:
That songs of praise be always on our lips:
That we strive to live as sisters and brothers
    to God's creation:
That all share alike in the bounty God gives:
That water be shared in its goodness:
That artists be challenged and supported
    by our community:
That scientists seek the healing of the earth:
That chemists and physicists delight
    in creation's beauty:
That those who practice the arts of healing be
    blessed in their work:
That those who raise crops treat the earth
    with reverence:
That the poisoned places be made clean again:

That commerce be for the good of all:
That the earth may be the good household
of all its creatures:

LORD'S PRAYER

CLOSING PRAYER

Not to us, O Lord, not to us,
but to you be glory in your creation.
Give us time to savor your beauty.
Give us touch and taste,
smell and sight and hearing
to call creation good, to share all with all,
and to give you thanks in Jesus,
who is Lord for ever and ever.
~*Amen.*

BLESSING

May the compassionate and merciful God
give us a restful night
and peace at the last.
~*Amen.*

SIGN OF PEACE